Praise for *The Good Life*

With Trip having such a transcultural platform and influence, I'm grateful that his writings on the essence of a good life are available. He gives potent insight on finding satisfaction in God alone, redefines what most people view as good, and unveils what God defines as a truly good life. Get it. Read it.

–LECRAE, *Grammy-nominated rap artist and co-owner of Reach Records*

Fresh and faithful. Fun and filling.

–MARK DEVER, *senior pastor, Capitol Hill Baptist Church, Washington, D.C., and author of* Nine Marks of a Healthy Church

My entire ministry has been focused on speaking to my generation. As I struggle with my concerns for the next one, Trip Lee erases my worries with this brilliant body of work. Inside each chapter speaks a young man who cares about the streets as well as protecting the Holy Scriptures. I am proud to know truth will continue through Trip Lee.

–KIRK FRANKLIN, *Grammy-winning gospel artist*

Trip Lee has been worth listening to for some time. Now we know he is worth reading too. This brief book is an excellent introduction to the Christian faith, communicated in a way that is authentic and accessible. I'm thankful for this wonderful brother, for his humility, for his theological conviction, and for his growing influence. Most of all, I'm thankful for the way he points me to the glory of God and the gospel of Jesus Christ.

–KEVIN DEYOUNG, *senior pastor at University Reformed Church, Lansing, Michigan, and author of* Just Do Something

The Good Life is not a silly book about how to get whatever you might wish for in this life. Nor is it a book about how to become rich and famous . . . or even a well-known Christian rap artist. It's a beautiful retelling of the simple gospel story: that all we need is found in our Savior, and all the suffering and waiting for heaven we do in this world is nothing in comparison to the good life that is given us freely in Christ. Our idols will never satisfy us; the good things in our lives were never meant to be our gods, they were meant to tell us that there is something more. *The Good Life* is a really good book. Buy one for yourself and buy some to give away to friends who need to hear the good news again.

–**ELYSE FITZPATRICK,** *author of* Because He Loves Me: How Christ Transforms Our Daily Life

Knowledgeable and personable. Witty and insightful. Serious and joyful. Trip Lee makes a wonderful tour guide to the good life. You'd expect a rapper to be a proponent of all that's worldly and materialistic. Not this rapper. Lee explores rival worldviews and points us to that one truly good life established by the only One who is good. Read and discover what's good.

–**THABITI ANYABWILE,** *senior pastor of First Baptist Church of Grand Cayman, Cayman Islands, and author of* The Gospel for Muslims

Trip represents the gracious movement of God in the church, calling a new generation to a very old message. Trip is both a skilled communicator and capable theologian, and I gladly commend both this book, and his ministry. What would it look like for Jesus to be Lord of the hip-hop culture? You'll catch a glimpse of it in this book.

–**J.D. GREEAR,** *pastor of The Summit Church, Durham, North Carolina, and author of* Gospel: Recovering the Power that Made Christianity Revolutionary

The Good Life is like an alarm clock that awakens you to a whole new way of thinking about life. Trip has done an amazing job of giving us a relevant and revolutionary approach to finding the good life.

–BRYAN CARTER, *senior pastor of Concord Church, Dallas, Texas*

The Good Life is one the most culturally intelligent, biblically saturated presentations of what God intends for men and women that American Christianity has produced in decades. Lee is masterful at applying the scope of the gospel to the idols and disordered loves that tempt all of us to distrust the goodness of God. *The Good Life* will enrich those who are mature believers as well as those investigating the claims of Christ for the first time.

–ANTHONY B. BRADLEY, *associate professor of Theology and Ethics at The King's College and author of* Liberating Black Theology

Thankfully there are some clear, biblical, and prophetic voices coming from Christian hip-hop. Trip Lee is one of them. In this book, Trip reminds us that we serve a good God who intends good for His people. This book on the good life is a good read.

–ANTHONY CARTER, *lead pastor of East Point Church, East Point, Georgia, and author of* Black and Reformed

THE GOOD LIFE

THE GOOD LIFE TRIP LEE

MOODY PUBLISHERS

CHICAGO

All Scripture quotations, unless otherwise indicated, are taken from *The Holy Bible, English Standard Version*. Copyright © 2000, 2001 by Crossway Bibles, a division of Good News Publishers. Used by permission. All rights reserved.

Scripture quotations marked (NIV) are taken from the Holy Bible, New International Version®, NIV®. Copyright © 1973, 1978, 1984 by Biblica, Inc.™ Used by permission of Zondervan. All rights reserved worldwide. www.zondervan.com.

Edited by Bailey Utecht
Cover design: Greg Lutze
Cover layout: Alex Medina
Interior design: Smartt Guys design
Author Photo: Matt Hawthorne/Matt Hawthorne Photography

Quotation or citation of song lyrics does not imply author or publisher endorsement of the entire work.

ISBN: 978-0-8024-0858-7

We hope you enjoy this book from Moody Publishers. Our goal is to provide high-quality, thought-provoking books and products that connect truth to your real needs and challenges. For more information on other books and products written and produced from a biblical perspective, go to www.moodypublishers.com or write to:

Moody Publishers
820 N. La Salle Boulevard
Chicago, IL 60610

1 3 5 7 9 10 8 6 4 2

Printed in the United States of America

DEDICATION

To my son, Q. I'm praying you'll live the good life.

CONTENTS

INTRODUCTION

EVERYBODY WANTS TO LIVE the good life. No one says, "No thanks, I'll take a bad life instead." Instead, we spend our lives pursuing what we think is best. By "the good life," we usually mean the best possible life we could live. The life that leads to the most fulfillment, happiness, and success. Why wouldn't we want to live this kind of life?

As a child, if you would have asked me to paint a picture of the good life, my answer probably would have been typical. It would've revolved around money, pleasure, success, and respect. I think that's the picture that most of us would paint, because that's what we've been taught. But I think there's something better. That's why I've written this book.

Some of you might be thinking, "How can this guy tell me how to live the good life? We all have our own paths." Well, the good life I'm talking about doesn't change from person to person. The good life I'm talking about is the same for all of us. I define the good life as "living by faith in a good God." I hope you'll see what I mean as you read the book.

As you may have already guessed, I'm a Christian. Not because some screaming preacher forced it on me, but because I believe the words that Jesus said. So my understanding of the good life isn't based on my own ideas or experiences. It's based on what God has said in His Word.

I will tell personal stories, and I will interact with the culture, but I'm also going to use the Bible a lot. I don't think using the Bible means it has to be boring though, so I've tried to write in an engaging way. I don't consider myself the expert on how to live well. But I think I know the One who is, so I'm going to talk about Him in every chapter.

I split the discussion into four sections. Section one asks the question, "What is the good life?" Section two talks about the keys to living the good life. Section three asks the question, "How do I live the good life?" And finally, section four addresses what kind of good we can expect from God.

The robot image you see on the cover is meant to point to something meaningful. Robots are those who are still controlled by lies. I put a slash through that robot because I believe we can be freed to live in light of the truth. I hope this book will point you in the right direction. Without further ado, welcome to the good life.

WHAT IS THE GOOD LIFE?

DON'T EAT THE FRUIT

I WAS ELEVEN YEARS OLD. I was sitting on the floor in my bedroom, shoes off and headphones blaring. There was nowhere else I'd rather be than in my space, with my music. The deep bass piercing my eardrums was supplied by Jay-Z's *Vol. 2, The Hard Knock Life*, my favorite album at the time.

On track fourteen, Jigga and JD brag, "In the Ferrari and Jaguar switching four lanes, top down, screaming out money ain't a thing."[1] Yes, I had the clean version, so my ears were shielded from the foul language, but not from all harm. There is no edited version that removes worldviews.

What I thought was just fun music was actually far more. When I hit play on my portable CD player, I was going to class. They weren't teaching me math and grammar, but they were teaching me how to view the world. They were lecturing me about what my aspirations should be, and what is most important in the world. And unknowingly, I was a star pupil. I ate it up and believed the lie that Ferraris and Jaguars are what life is largely about. If I wanted the good life, I needed the money, the cars, and the girls.

Rappers weren't my only teachers though. I heard lessons every day from my parents, my schoolteachers, my friends, and my favorite TV shows. Every day I was bombarded with messages and images that shaped my perspective on life. And I'm not alone. Every single one of us has an idea about what "the good life" is, and we've learned it from somewhere. In the same way our region dictates the accent we speak with, our environments and influences shape our ideas about life.

Every time you hear an idea or observe a behavior, you're being presented with a message. And as we take those messages in, we can either reject or accept them (though we often do this subconsciously). We shouldn't be asking whether or not we're being taught; there's no question about that. We should be asking whether or not we're being taught well.

WE'VE BEEN LIED TO

I know we're just getting started, but can I be brutally honest for a moment? I think we've been lied to. No one wants to be deceived, but we have and we didn't even notice it. They told us that the good life means seeking our own happiness at all costs. They taught us that our goal should be a life free from any worries. And we believed them.

But we've been duped. They sold us materialism disguised as determination. They led us to counterfeit satisfaction at the expense of the real thing. They told us to center ourselves on ourselves. And when we asked if there was another way, they whispered in our ear an assured yet deceitful, "Absolutely not." We've been deceived. We have eaten the fruit.

But who is "they"? Who lied to us and why?

THE LIARS

We have three great enemies in this life: the world, the flesh, and the Devil. The Devil is God's great adversary. He doesn't have horns, he doesn't carry a pitchfork, and he doesn't own hell. But he does have a lot of influence in our world. In fact, he has so much sway that the apostle Paul refers to him as "the prince of the power of the air" (Ephesians 2:2). He is constantly feeding lies to whoever will receive them. The Bible calls him "the father of lies" (John 8:44).

The "world" is the system that supports and distributes his lies. "World" refers to the system and method of operation among sinful man. This world system is controlled by the Devil and it leads us away from the truth. And the "flesh" is our fallen, sinful nature. Our flesh receives and believes

Gal 5:15-17

these lies. Something has gone wrong inside of us, so our hearts have an appetite for falsehood (we'll talk about what's gone wrong a little later). Instead of rejecting these lies, our fleshly taste buds crave them. The result of this devastating world, flesh, and Devil trifecta is that all of us have aligned ourselves with false ideas about how we should live.

And unfortunately, we've allowed our enemies to control us like we're their little robots. They've told us how to live and we've done as we were told. But we don't have to be robots. We can be freed, and live like we were made to live, but not until we stop believing lies.

This is humanity's greatest problem; it's not sickness or natural disasters. It's that we believe the lies of the enemy over the truth of God. This is what happened with Adam in the garden, this is what happened with God's people in the wilderness, and this is what keeps us from living the good life today.

A GREAT FALL

Genesis tells us the story of Adam and Eve, the first man and woman, created in the image and likeness of almighty God. They're not characters in a fairy tale; they're our oldest relatives. They were created to be connected to God, to be satisfied by Him, and to obey Him. In love, God breathed life into them and gave them dominion over the Earth. But He also gave them boundaries.

"And the Lord God commanded the man, saying, 'You may surely eat of every tree of the garden, but of the tree of the knowledge of good and evil you shall not eat, for in the day that you eat of it you shall surely die'"(Genesis 2: 16–17).

God's goodness is on display here as He gives them access to every tree in the garden—except one. But God doesn't restrict their access because He wants to keep them from the best fruit. God gives them this command because He loves them. It is for their good. Adam and Eve would have lived a life free from any hardship, shame, or worry if they had trusted God's good commands for them. But they didn't.

Flip over to Genesis 3. This is where Satan, influencing the serpent, first sowed the poisonous seeds of doubt that infect us to this day. His deception is threefold. He questions the content of God's words, he questions the truthfulness of God's words, and he questions the motives behind God's words.

He says to Eve, "Did God actually say, 'You shall not eat of any tree in the garden' . . . You will not surely die. For God knows that when you eat of it your eyes will be opened, and you will be like God, knowing good and evil" (Genesis 3:1b, 4–5). After making them doubt God's trustworthiness, he sets an alternate reward before them, namely, becoming like God. Ironically, Adam and Eve were the one part of creation that was created in the likeness of God. But instead of trusting God, Adam and Eve took the bait and ate the fruit.

This is the most devastating event in human history. The problem wasn't that Adam and Eve ate fruit. Fruit is a good gift from God. The problem was that they ate the wrong fruit. Instead of enjoying the fruit God gave them to enjoy, they disobeyed and went after the fruit that would destroy them. They believed the serpent when he suggested that God gave them boundaries to keep them from good things.

We're being fed those same lies today. The world is casting doubt on God and His Word, but will we take the bait? Will we believe the lies?

THE USUAL SUSPECTS

Every day we're being fed a variety of lies about living the good life, and most of them fit into at least one of these three categories:

1. Hedonism

This is a thousand-dollar word that basically means seeing your own happiness and pleasure as the most important thing in life. Most people would never actually say that their happiness and pleasure are the highest good, but they don't have to. Their words reveal it and their actions show it. When they say things like, "Just do whatever makes you happy," their perspective is on full display.

Many of us value our own happiness and pleasure far above everything else, and this value guides all of our decisions. We just want to be pleased. Most people think rappers and rock stars are the only hedonists, but that's not the case. Hedonism doesn't always look like a life full of drugs and sex; sometimes it looks like a life full of comfort and laziness. This lie basically tells us to do whatever it takes to be happy.

2. All-you-can-be-ism

This lie can be deceptive because it seems more sophisticated and noble. Just be the best you that you can be. This lie says the greatest thing you can do is "make it out the hood." Or maybe "Do well in school so you can go to college, so you can get that job, so you can reach that status, so you can get that promotion," and so on. The highest good in this view is achievement. The end goal is greatness. So do whatever it takes to be the best you can be.

3. It's-all-about-me-ism

This worldview expects everyone, including God, to focus on us. It teaches us that the good life means feeling loved by all those around us. It teaches us to do whatever it takes to get the respect of our peers. Everyone else is here to affirm us and give us what we want.

This worldview gets even more dangerous when it's distributed by religious people. It says that we should dream big and believe God to give us whatever we desire, because that's what God does. It says that if we obey God, He will fix all of our problems in this life. This lie makes God your servant, instead of the other way around. It tells us that God will do whatever it takes to give us what we want, if we will only believe in Him and obey Him.

There really isn't much difference between these three lies. They have a core value in common: self. They are world-views built around the idol of ME. But there is a way to live life that centers on God rather than me. The problem is that none of us naturally pursue that way of life. Every one of us has bought into the lies.

If we're going to live the good life, we can't be robots. When we turn on the TV or walk around our neighborhoods, we see a lot of clones. We see beautiful people made in God's image whose lives have been marked by faith in falsehoods. We'll see the same thing if we take an honest look in the mirror. But none of us have to be robots. We can be freed, and begin to live the way we were created to live. We can stop spiraling down and start living it up.

FIXING THE PROBLEM

Recently, I watched the movie *Limitless*. The movie centers on a young man who is full of potential but has sabotaged every chance he has. He's a good writer, but his book deal is about to disappear because he hasn't written a single word in months. His creative wells have dried up, he just lost his long-time girlfriend, and he drinks far too much alcohol. So how do these problems get solved?

He meets an old friend who introduces him to a new, revolutionary drug. It allows him to use 100 percent of his brain function, and with this increased brain function, his whole life changes. Not only does his creativity explode, but he becomes a better person; he's a hard worker, he's no longer a drunk, and he wins back his girlfriend. And all of this because he can think clearly now and make the right decisions.

Wouldn't you like to have this pill that could magically fix your life? It sure sounds like an easy path to the good life. I really enjoyed the movie, but it obviously isn't meant to be very realistic. Aside from the fact that a pill like this will likely never exist, the storyline builds on false assumptions. Even if someone did create such a pill, it would never have the same effect on us. Yes, maybe we would be more creative, and maybe we would become the most capable in whatever field we chose, but it could never do anything to fix our laziness, unreliability, and drunkenness.

A pill that allows us to think clearer could never help us to make all of the right decisions because our main problem is not rational, it's spiritual. The people who think the most clearly and rationally are still born sinful. We love our sin. We choose to disobey God, not because we don't think clearly enough, but because we don't love, value, or trust God enough. We need to be freed from bondage to sin, and no percentage of brain function can do that. We need new hearts.

But we can't go in for surgery if we don't realize we're sick. No one likes to be lied to, but until we recognize that our hearts are ill and that we've been living in light of lies we will continue walking off the cliff. Proverbs 14:12 says, "There is a way that seems right to a man, but its end is the way to death."

These lies promised the good life, but in reality they only kept us from it and led us to death. We need a better teacher.

LYRICS FROM "ROBOT"

Hey I was born "less than human," I know it sounds crazy
But I was really born a robot as a baby
No real life in me, I just played my role
No self-control, I just did what I was told
I got my first order, I was just a day old
But I didn't have a chance 'cause my heart was way cold
My heart took the orders, it couldn't break the mold
I was sold under bondage and I couldn't take control
So I was just chillin' in my robot clothes
With my robot friends and my robot flow
Livin' robot ways 'cause that's all I know
Till I heard I could be freed from my robot soul.[2]

2

THE GOOD TEACHER

I'M TERRIBLE WITH DIRECTIONS. Anybody who knows me well knows that I have an uncanny ability to get lost anywhere. It's almost like God decided He would humble me by maturing me twenty-plus years but leaving me with a five-year-old's sense of direction. It's hard to be proud when you often get lost five blocks from your own house. So whenever someone asks me for directions I automatically default to my wife, who seems like she was born with a built-in Google Maps app.

One time, while I was living in Philly, my friend and I were taking a trip to New York to do an interview at a radio station. It just so happens that this friend was horrible with directions too. As soon as we got on the road, he looked to me and asked if I knew how to get there. This was a disaster waiting to happen.

What should have been a two-hour trip ended up being a five-hour trip, and regrettably the same thing happened on the way back. We really should have printed out directions beforehand and asked our wives to assist us. But instead it was like two blind dudes getting together and trading opinions about the Mona Lisa. Neither of us could help the other out. We were hopeless.

Well, this is kind of what it's like when human beings trade opinions about what the good life is. All of us have been duped into believing lies, and all of us have defective hearts. Our hearts are like the GPS of our entire being, but they are broken and always lead us in the wrong direction. So instead of following our hearts, or following other people with broken hearts, we need to follow someone who is trustworthy. Sure, human beings won't always lead you astray, but is there anyone we can trust to give us the truth every time?

THE GOOD TEACHER

The truth is that the God of the Universe is the only one who can truly lead us to the good life. I know saying that God is the best teacher may sound clichéd or even ancient to many of us. We're in an advanced day and age, and it's hard to take our cues from ideas that seem so old. I know there are some who think, "Why should I trust God? What has He ever done for me?" God has allowed most of us to go through deeply painful times in our lives. Plus, He doesn't even live on Earth. He's up there in the clouds somewhere, right? What could He possibly know about our lives? Well I want you to hear me out, and let me tell you a few reasons why I think He's trustworthy—far more than us and others.

WHO HE IS

For one, He is God. That statement in itself says more about Him than anything else could. He is the all-powerful Creator, Sustainer, and Owner of all things, including you and me. All of the universe belongs to Him. And the fact that He made every inch of creation makes Him the authority on how it should operate.

In 1891 James Naismith was asked to create an indoor game for the students at a university. He racked his brain and came up with a new, unique game he called "basket ball." He grabbed a soccer ball, hung up two peach baskets, and posted thirteen rules on the wall for the young men to see. They were ready to play their first game.

Now can you imagine one of the students arguing with him about what the rules were? It would be arrogant and downright silly. How could they tell Mr. Naismith how to play the game he created? Similarly, God is our Creator, He has given us life, and He knows how it's supposed to work. How arrogant of us to think for a moment that we know better.

I imagine that if the students were left to themselves to figure out the game, they would have come up with a much less glorious version—throwing the ball at one another and pulling the peach baskets down. Left to our sinful imaginations, human beings will not come up with the right way to live. We'll spend our energies chasing fantasies and masquerades, blinded to the true realities of life. God's way is not only right, it's better. Using your life for hedonism is like using a Ferrari for target practice. Not only do you rob that life of its higher calling, but you destroy it in the process. God the Father knows best.

In addition to that, God's identity gives Him ownership over His creation. Psalm 24 says, "The Earth is the Lord's, and everything in it, the world, and all who live in it; for he founded it on the seas and established it on the waters" (NIV). That includes us.

Most of us live under the illusion that our lives belong to us, and us alone. But the truth is, you belong to your Creator. He made us, therefore we're His. It's that simple. This doesn't mean we're just objects, lacking any kind of freedom. But it does mean that rejecting God's leadership is robbing Him of something that is rightfully His.

Not to mention, He is the highest authority. There is no one He has to answer to. He did not have to be elected and He cannot be impeached. His judgments cannot be appealed and His decrees don't have to be approved by any council. He will never lose power and His term will never come to an end. He is God!

WHAT HE'S LIKE

Secondly, He is good. No one wants to follow an evil leader. Putting someone's character into question casts doubt on their ability to lead well.

Can you think of how many times a trusted public leader has had a moral failing? Can you think of how the public reacted? The scandal always erupts and the media has a field day. Whether it be a religious figure or political figure, their leadership is no longer trusted. They lose the credibility they need to play their role. These days it's hard for the public to trust anyone. Emerging new leaders seem so promising, but it seems like it's just a matter of time before some scandal comes out.

Well, we can be sure that scandalous reports of God's moral failing will never surface. There's nothing to report! Psalm 145:17 says that, "The Lord is righteous in all his ways and kind in all his works."

This means that if somehow you were able to investigate and comb through His ways and His works for the past thousand years, you would find nothing but goodness. You could examine His record for the past million years and you would find nothing but perfect, pure, uncorrupted righteousness. A quick glance through the Old and New Testaments would show how He's perfectly led His people for thousands of years. And this is what we can expect from Him in the future.

Now contrast that with you and me. If someone were to comb through our actions for even the past day, they would find plenty of unrighteousness. They would likely find pride, or dishonesty, or lust, or all of the above. The decay in our hearts is exposed by the death in our actions. Yet, we insist on following our own intuition over God's proven, good leadership.

We should find comfort in the fact that God is incapable of leading us in the wrong direction. His counsel has never been unwise and His perspective has never been mistaken. His moral compass has never been off-kilter and He's never had to apologize. His character and His leadership are picture-perfect, which should motivate us to enthusiastically follow Him to the good life.

WHAT HE DESIRES

Lastly, we should follow Him because He desires good for us. God created you and He wants you to live the good life. Sometimes we imagine that God is some sort of ornery old man who's always in a bad mood and frowns upon good times. We've allowed our culture to paint Him as a sort of joy police, sniffing out happiness. This couldn't be further from the truth. God is happy, and He loves everything that is good.

In fact, He is the designer of all good things. They were His ideas. In his letter to scattered Christians, James reminds us that "Every good gift and every perfect gift is from above, coming down from the Father of lights" (James 1:17). Think for a moment about some of the good things you enjoy— your favorite meal, hilarious jokes, your best friends—there is no other person that can be credited for inventing those good things. God thought them up, God created them, and God gave them to you.

He has given countless good gifts to enjoy. But why does God have so many "rules" if He wants us to live the good life? It's because His good gifts can only be rightly enjoyed in their proper contexts. When we rip them away from the context they were made to function in, we corrupt them. This may seem like a cop-out but we apply this principle naturally to other things all the time. Windex: good for windows, bad for an ice-cold drink. Guns: good for honest law enforcement, bad for gangsters. Outlets function well for charging iPhones, but they don't function so well as finger puppets. When placed in the hands of sinners, good things can go bad pretty easily.

The main danger with good things is that our hearts always

grab hold of them and forget where they came from. Instead of praising God for His good creation, we forget He's there, and just praise the creation instead. That's why we think God is evil when He gives us boundaries. But these precious boundaries keep us from praising the pages and ignoring the author.

Despite what I've said above, some of you still don't believe that God wants good for us. You feel like there's not enough proof. Well there's no greater proof than the fact that He sent His Son to die so that we could begin to live. This is the single greatest display of goodness in the history of the world, and we'll talk about it more in the chapters to come. For now, I want you to consider who's a better leader of your life. You? Your friends? Or this God we've been thinking about?

FOLLOW THE LEADER

While we do have the freedom to choose who we will follow, there is only One who we were *made* to follow. No matter where we live, how old we are, or how wealthy we are, there is only one Lord of all. We need to define "good" the way God defines it. Otherwise, we will call something a "good life" that's not good at all.

God has graciously offered to lead us to the good life. The road isn't short, and it isn't easy, but the destination is well worth it. Will you follow Him there?

LYRICS FROM "ROBOT"

I was still a drone, nothing but a clone
I only knew the lies, 'cause that's all that I was shown
But I've been remade, my heart is no longer stone
Where my ex-robots who can sing this song?
Now I've been remade and I'm no longer hollow

A real man came, changed everything that I know
He gave me truth, that's a hard pill to swallow
He gave me new commands, and He freed me up to follow.[1]

3

A NEW DEFINITION

GROWING UP, I HAD ONE SIBLING, a sister, and I loved her dearly, but I always wished I had a brother too. I wanted somebody I could do male stuff with—someone I could shove, and wrestle, and punch. You don't punch girls or you get punched (at least that was the case in my house). So I thought, "Maybe she'll play basketball with me," but she never wanted to play. One day when I was feeling pretty desperate, I swallowed my pride and agreed to make a trade: one game of Barbies in exchange for a game of basketball in the backyard. She accepted my offer and I played with Barbies that day, little voices and all. I didn't want to play with Barbies, I was just enduring for the sake of a nice, masculine game of hoops.

Well, it turns out I got tricked. When it was finally time

to play basketball I mustered up all the maleness I had left in me and headed for the back door. But instead of racing to the door behind me, my big sister nonchalantly said, "I don't really wanna play anymore." I'm sure my little eyes bugged all the way out of my head and my jaw dropped to my sternum. I thought, "I just sacrificed my young-manhood for nothing!?" It was a sad day.

But why did I agree to do something so embarrassing in the first place? It's simple. I believed that playing with Barbies would earn me a game of basketball. I had faith in her promise, but she changed her mind. I'm not the only one who makes decisions this way though.

As human beings we make all of our decisions based on what we believe in that moment. If I believe the road is blocked, I'll take a detour. If I believe a movie will be good, I'll take my wife to see it. We all live by faith. Whether or not we live the good life depends on what we have faith in. *The good life is living by faith in a good God.*

WHAT DOES IT MEAN?

This means more than just believing that God exists. There are plenty of people all over the world who believe in God's existence, but that faith doesn't make much difference in their lives. Their belief in God's existence doesn't impact their lives any more than my belief in the existence of Kobe

Bryant. Yes, I believe he's real, but it doesn't change anything about my lifestyle. He's out there somewhere, but what does that have to do with the choices I make every day?

I'll tell you what does impact our daily choices, though: our faith in the benefits of being liked. We want to be liked, so we try to fit in. Or, maybe our faith in the pleasures of sex; we want to experience that pleasure, so we pursue that closeness with someone. My question for you is: does your belief in God impact your daily life? Does it impact how you work, or how you interact with others? If not, then maybe you haven't begun to live by faith in the right stuff. Faith itself is not a virtue. Faith is only a virtue when you believe on something that can hold you up.

Faith in your Creator means more than giving lip service to His existence. It means believing what He says and so ordering your life around it. It means inconveniencing yourself for the sake of following Him. The Lord said, "Blessed . . . are those who hear the word of God and keep it!" (Luke 11:28). Our old conceptions of the good life must be replaced with this new one. Faith in the God of eternity must crowd out faith in promises of futility.

EXPOSING THE LIES

This new picture of the good life probably seems kind of ordinary and basic. At first glance it does sound a little less glorious than most of the other ideas we've heard. But are the other ones really better?

Take for example a tweet that popped up on my timeline the other day. It said, "The greatest pleasure in life is doing what people say you cannot do." Really? Of course everyone gets a little bit of joy from proving the haters and naysayers wrong, but is that really the "greatest pleasure in life"? If we allow this perspective to motivate our lives, we might be very successful, but we'll be terribly let down when we finally reach that goal. What happens when we prove that last naysayer wrong and find that we still have issues? This is classic all-you-can-be-ism, and it is not the good life.

Let's take another example: on his hit song "Good Life" Kanye West boasts, "So I roll through good, Y'all pop the trunk, I pop the hood—Ferrari, And she got the goods, and she got that [butt], I got to look, sorry . . . if they hate then let 'em hate and watch the money pile up, the good life."[1]

As you know, hip-hop is always good for a heavy dose of hedonism. The images slowly seduce us and draw us in. I know this is the picture I was chasing after: Coke bottle figures and seven-figure checks. But what happens when you get there? Even the most beautiful women are imperfect and let us down from time to time. And surely, shiny machines rolling on wheels can't be what we were made to live for. They break down, they get dented in accidents, and they eventually go to the same junkyard as Hyundais. Surely we can do better. This is not the good life.

How about this sermon I heard the other day. The preacher stepped onto the stage before a sea of young people and shouted, "A lot of y'all wonder why things never go your way. What you need to do is submit to God and He'll start blessing you. If you want those blessings you've been hoping for, you need to start following God's commands. Walk up to the front and start to receive your blessings." Here is a clear picture of religious All-about-me-ism.

At first it sure sounds like the good life. Do what God says and things will start going your way. The problem with this is God never said He'd do that! This view basically uses God instead of believing God. It says to attach yourself to Him in hopes of receiving the things that the other lies promise: pleasure and success. Sure, God has promised to bless those who follow Him by faith, but He didn't promise everything would go your way. And He didn't promise that all those blessings would come all at once. So what happens when we start trying to do what God says and yet, life is still tough sometimes? Empty promises and crushed expectations can't be what the good life is really all about.

THE PROBLEMS

These lies have a couple main problems.

One, they don't keep their word. They promise a lot, but

they don't deliver. Their benefits either don't exist or they don't last. They offer sixty or seventy years of pleasure instead of pleasures forevermore. Why would I spend my life in pursuit of temporary or imaginary goals instead of real, eternal ones? It's a waste of time. The lies we've been told teach us to shoot for the ground instead of the stars, and sadly we're right on target. Our aim is too low. I like how the Proverbs put it: "There is a way that seems right to a man, but its end is the way to death" (Proverbs 14:12).

Two, the lies center around us. They're so subjective. Do whatever makes you happy. Do whatever brings you success. Do what it takes to get your blessing. It's all about you. But haven't we been made for something bigger? Scripture answers that question with a definitive YES! Colossians 1:16b reminds us that "all things were created through him and for him." You were made for something—I should say someone—infinitely bigger than yourself.

When we reject God's plan and demand that our lives be all about us, we insult Him and attempt to rip Him off His throne. This would be like our iPods rejecting our uploaded music and demanding that we sync some music that they want to play. We would probably throw them out. Why? Because iPods exist to be used for our purposes, not the other way around. This is the worst kind of confusion. The good life must be bigger than you and me.

Three, the lies are out of reach for most of the world. We should be suspicious of any "good life" that only well-off people could ever reach. An overwhelming majority of the people on Earth will never get anywhere close to rich. And they can't afford to live under the illusion that God will give them everything they want right now. They just hope to have food and water on the table. Maybe they don't have the means or opportunities to make it out the hood, or to climb any kind of corporate ladder. They just want to do their job and get by.

The real good life, on the other hand, is available to all. No one is exempt—black or white, rich or poor, tall or short, healthy or sick—everyone can live the good life. In fact, we were created to live it.

CATCH THE VISION

My brother-in-law is twenty-seven years old. He's an intelligent man with natural leadership abilities. He earned his college degree and could probably succeed in whatever field he put his mind to. Charismatic men like him excel in their fields, rise to the top, and live long, successful lives. But he had something else in mind.

He's built his life around leaving the comforts of US soil that he might serve the needy in another country. Currently, he's working an entry-level desk job, trying to pay off school loans before he goes overseas. Some may look at him and think, "Poor guy. His life doesn't seem all that great." But I think they're wrong. My brother-in-law is living the good life! When the time is right he's going to leave his comforts behind and lay down his life for the sake of others. I think he caught the vision. We don't have to be a missionary like he is, but we should be inspired by his desire to live by faith in his Maker.

Or how about one of my artist friends. He's a very popular musician and is known worldwide for his one-of-a-kind artistry. He's sold tons of albums and toured both nationally and internationally. Though wealth has never been his goal, he's earned his fair share of dollar bills over the years. He could have spent his money on a bunch of cars, a mansion with more rooms than he could use, and a bunch of jewelry. But instead, he used his money to help start a nonprofit to support the vision of his church, and to help other artists make good music.

More than that, I've witnessed several occasions where he turned down offers for appearances that would garner him even more fame and notoriety. Material things and popularity made big promises, but he chose to believe the promises of God instead. It seems like my friend has caught the vision. His faith is in God.

The good life doesn't mean we get everything we want. The good life is belief in God even when we don't get what we want. The good life doesn't mean we live whatever way feels best to us. It means we live how we were created to live. The good life isn't the high life. The good life is the life that's been laid down. Have you caught the vision?

STARTING TO LIVE IT

So that's it then, right? I just start having faith in God and doing what He says. Unfortunately it's not so simple, because deep inside, part of us doesn't want the good life. We want the "now" life. Our eyes are blind to true goodness. Our hands and feet are shackled by falsehoods. Our hearts are hardened stones that refuse to be molded.

The good life is more than just making the decision. A broken human being just deciding to live the good life is like a paralyzed man just deciding to walk again. There's something wrong with our whole being. In order to live right, we have to start all over again. We need a remix, a comeback, a rebirth. We need a Savior.

So in the next section we'll begin to explore how we can be rescued from bondage and set on the path of freedom.

LYRICS FROM "NEW DREAMS"

Hey I was raised in that lone star state, where we go hard
Can't do it small at all 'cause big things are at stake
My dreams as a buck was to make a large bank
Daddy told me be the best, no one can tell me I can't
Be the best baller, or be the best rapper
I got a little older and went after the latter
Grind till I shine, trying to climb that ladder
And grab a couple girls 'cause ya boy look dapper
But at a young age, I saw I had it wrong
Was full of drive but moving in reverse all along
Dreams full of pride, heart full of stone
You know I had to redefine what I grind on
Success is dangerous if you don't do it right
He gave us everything for pointing to Him right
So toast to the King who gave me some new dreams
Everything for His name, that's how I do things.[2]

KEYS TO THE GOOD LIFE

WELCOME TO **THE GOOD LIFE**

THE FIRST DAY OF SCHOOL is a unique phenomenon. It's pretty much the only time young people are excited to show up for class. I don't know about you, but school always tortured me, September through May. In spite of that, somehow I would find myself anticipating its return by the end of summer. There was something invigorating about showing up the first day back with new kicks, a new haircut, and new swag. I always felt like I had become so much cooler over that three month break, and all my peers needed to see it. The fact that I felt this way is probably proof that I wasn't so cool after all.

Of course my teachers were never very concerned about my coolness. They always showed up that first day with their own agendas. They had syllabi in hand, ready to commence the "torture." At least they were merciful enough to ease us in though. Day number one was usually the day for orientation. It was a day to say, "Welcome back and here's where we're going." Well I want you to consider these next three chapters your "good life orientation." I want to answer the question "How do we live the good life?" But we won't be able to build properly if the foundation isn't there.

So allow me to hand out the good life syllabi. There are three main areas we will discuss in this section. These three realities will give us a framework for this section, and more importantly, for a good life. The three key areas are: the Good News, the Good Book, and "Good" People. None of these can be talked about without the others. They are intertwined, inseparable, and indispensable parts of the good life. We'll begin with the good news.

THE GOOD NEWS

I GREW UP IN THE BIBLE BELT. There was no shortage of Christian stuff around me. Until I was a teenager, I think almost every person I knew was a professing Christian. I actually remember a time in fifth grade when a student said he wasn't a Christian and the entire classroom collectively gasped. The needle scratched and everyone's heads turned as if to say, "I didn't know these 'non-Christians' actually existed."

But here's the thing. Some of the professing Christians I knew really loved Jesus, and some of them didn't. Some of them attended a church gathering every week, and others didn't. Some lived moral lives, and others didn't. So, under-standably, I was pretty confused about what it actually meant to be a Christian. Does it mean you go to church? Does it mean you are a nice person? I needed clarity.

When I was about five or six, I repeated a prayer after a children's pastor. This prayer led me to believe that I had become a Christian. But when I look back, I don't think I had begun to follow Christ yet. Mainly because I hadn't really understood and embraced the good news. By most standards I was a "good kid," but I was far from living the good life.

My good life began when I understood and embraced the good news. So I think it's incredibly important that I share this good news with you. Consider me the reporter, and consider this a breaking story. If we ignore it, we can never live the good life, but if we hear it and respond in faith, true life will begin.

WHAT GOOD NEWS?

Every time I turn on the TV, I hear horrific reports; news anchors tell us about the latest scandals, court cases, and natural disasters. The good stories seem outnumbered by the bad ones. But it's not because the news organizations are conspiring to keep us depressed. This is the reality of life in our broken world. There is more heartbreak than joy, more reason for grieving than rejoicing. I wonder if there's any good news out there.

Let's recap. In the first section, we explored the character and trustworthiness of God. We talked about who He is and what He's like. Our Creator exudes flawless beauty and perfection. All the people we know have some good traits and some bad traits, but not God. He's 100 percent pure goodness. We've never seen anybody or anything like Him.

In the first section we also talked about ourselves. We said that we are just like our great-grandfather Adam. His sin has brought a kind of curse upon all of us (Romans 5). If you still don't believe me, take a look at all of our lives. We all do bad things, even though we know it's wrong. Even as young children our sin is there. Think about it. You don't have to teach kids how to lie, something within them just knows how. Our sinful hearts are naturally bent toward disobedience. Adam's sin was a great tragedy, but we've followed right in his footsteps.

So we've established that God is perfect, and we're far from it. But what does all this mean? Should we just accept that we're different than God and move on? Let's talk about what our sin means to a holy God.

GOD THE JUDGE

Many people think of God as a nice guy in the sky who watches over us. They think He's probably somewhere hovering on a cloud, while angels feed Him grapes and fan Him with their wings. Perhaps He sees our sin and He doesn't like it, but He can't really pay it any attention. He's not concerned with the little details of our day-to-day lives. He has bigger things to worry about, like world peace and natural disasters. But if we ever need anything from Him, we can just take a second and throw up a prayer. He's sure to listen closely, and He might even grant us our wish if we're lucky.

This picture couldn't be further from the truth. The word "holy" doesn't mean much to most of us, but it should. The Bible says God dwells in a "high and holy place" (Isaiah 57:15). It also says He "dwells in unapproachable light" (1 Timothy 6:16). He's so glorious and holy, that no one can look upon Him and live (Exodus 33:20). He's not just some nice guy in the clouds; He's the glorious, majestic, master of all creation.

Not only that. God is deeply concerned with how we live our lives. We may be living for the approval of friends or family, but they are not the ones we'll have to answer to at the end of our lives. God is our Judge.

So if you wanted to, you could get up right now and try to go rob a bank. You have the freedom to do that, but you probably won't. You're smart enough to know that if you get caught, you'll have to answer to the authorities. The justice system has the right to punish you for your crimes.

Well in a much greater fashion, each one of us has committed crimes against God. And we can't weasel our way out of getting caught. We've failed to keep God's holy standards and He is the Judge that we'll have to answer to. Punishment from the state could never compare to the furious judgment God will deal out to those who've offended Him.

We often take sin lightly, but God doesn't seem to. He's not indifferent to our disobedience. He doesn't just shrug his shoulders and move on. Look at what David says to God in Psalm 5:4, "For you are not a God who delights in wickedness; evil may not dwell with you." God will not allow sinful men to stand before Him. Their rebellion is an awful stench to His holy nostrils. God hates sin because it rejects His authority, and exalts man over God. Our stubborn insurrection will not be tolerated. We will be held accountable for our actions, unless we can find mercy. This is where the good news comes in.

THE GOSPEL

Throughout the entire Bible, we see a long story centered on the coming of the Savior. The good news centers on this Savior and I'm going to zoom in on how this news relates to sinners like you and me.

Paul the apostle summarizes what he calls "the gospel" in his letter to the Corinthians, reminding them that "Christ died for our sins in accordance with the Scriptures, that he was buried, that he was raised on the third day in accordance with the Scriptures, and that he appeared to Cephas, then to the twelve" (1 Corinthians 15:3–5).

I. In accordance with the Scriptures

God is not oblivious. He sees the brokenness in our world, and in the people He created. From the beginning He's had a plan to interrupt that brokenness and send the great Healer into our world. God told His people about this great plan and those who trusted Him looked forward to the day when the Hero would come. They knew they needed a Savior to right wrongs and save them from their sins.

They weren't the only ones who needed a Hero. No man or woman will experience true freedom without Him. Each of us is like a hopeless POW, held captive by a cruel terrorist regime. Until someone more powerful swoops in to rescue us, we'll be doomed and tortured at the hands of the enemy. We need a Savior.

"There is no other name under heaven given among men by which we must be saved" (Acts 4:12). The Savior's name is Jesus. When it was the right time, the eternal Son of God came to Earth. His glory was veiled and His power restrained, but He was still glorious and mighty. This divine Hero showed up and showed us how it was done. He epitomized the good life. He didn't believe lies like you and me, but He lived in light of the truth. He was perfect in every sense of the word. He was the man God's people had been waiting for.

But He didn't come down from His throne to escape some kind of eternal boredom; He had a mission to carry out. At the center of His mission was the heroic rescue of a band of rebels. Or as Paul puts it in 1 Timothy 1:15, "Christ Jesus came into the world to save sinners."

II. Christ died for our sins

Most of us have heard the story of Jesus before. And the part we know best is the crucifixion. There are four accounts of the life of Christ in the Bible, and toward the end, each of them tells the same story of His brutal, unjust execution.

The religious elite never liked Jesus very much. His miracles brought Him all the attention, and His authoritative teaching challenged the status quo. He was a troublemaker in their eyes. From the moment He stepped on to the scene, they were plotting to take His life. But God had a plan to take His life before any of these men were even born (Acts 4:27–28). God sent His Son on a "death mission" and He knew it. Jesus set out on this mission out of deep love for sinners, and He willingly laid His life down.

Romans 6:23 says, "For the wages of sin is death . . ." A wage is what you earn for your work. Well each of us has earned death with our works. Our sin has provoked a holy God, and our sentence is an eternal death penalty. Hell isn't a popular subject in our day, but the terrible punishment matches the terrible crimes we've committed.

I know what many of us are thinking at this point. "That's

harsh. I've never done anything that bad! Sure, I've lusted and lied, but those are small sins. But the truth is, as one man said it, that "There is no such thing as a small sin against a great God."[1] Our sin isn't a mere breaking of rules; it's an offense against a person. Any offense against a great God is a great offense. And it does deserve eternal death.

But the good news is that Jesus died so that we wouldn't have to. Romans 5:8 says, "God shows his love for us in that while we were still sinners, Christ died for us." Some of us doubt God and we want proof that He actually loves us. Well look no further. The death of Jesus is the greatest display of love in the history of the universe. No mother's love could compare to this love. No romantic love could compare to this love. Jesus' love for sinners is greater than we could imagine.

When the God-man was nailed to the cross, He wasn't dying His own death. He was dying our death. He suffered that cruel punishment so that sinners like you and me wouldn't have to pay for our own sins. Christ took that death so that we wouldn't have to. Or as Hebrews 2:9 puts it, "he [tasted] death for everyone."

Christ saw the chaos of sin and death in our world. So He invaded enemy territory and declared war. His enemies did capture and kill Him, but death was the very way He planned to give us life. It was by death that He defeated death for all those who would trust in Him.

Death is always tragic, but every biography still ends the

same way. No matter who it is—from Dr. King to Tupac—everybody's life story will end with their death. That is, every biography except one. Death is part of Jesus' story, but it's definitely not the end.

III. Christ was raised on the third day

I remember going to church with my family as a kid, and listening to the preacher passionately proclaim truth. Most of the time, I didn't understand what he was so excited about. I felt like he screamed almost the whole time, especially at the end when he would come to a powerful, melodic climax.

What confused me most though, was that he (and all the other preachers) seemed to end with the same point every Sunday. It would go something like this, "They put Him on that cross, He hung His head, and He died. And Friday night, He was still in the grave. Saturday morning, my Lord was still dead. Saturday night, you guessed it; He was still in the tomb. But early! (Cue cheers from the congregation.) Early! ('Yeah!') Early Sunday morning He got up! ('Yeah!') He is risen!" At this point I would be looking around, confused and hungry, hoping the celebration didn't last too long.

But now I understand what all that commotion was about. Jesus' resurrection is worth celebrating! With His death He proved that He was who He said He was. He defeated death for us! There would be no good news if Christ was still in the grave. That "death mission" God sent Jesus on proved to be a "life mission." He rose, and offers life to all.

IV. Christ appeared

Resurrection sure sounds weird. This is one of the main reasons Christianity is mocked by skeptics. Suggesting that a man rose from the dead isn't consistent with nature and can't be proved by science. This has led many so-called Christians to deny the resurrection themselves. But we can't throw out the parts of Scripture that we don't like or understand.

So how do we know that He rose? Well for one, a bunch of people saw Him. Paul says He appeared to Peter, the other apostles, and five hundred other people! And when he wrote that letter, some of those eyewitnesses were still alive. Shai Linne says in his song, "Jesus Is Alive," "Imagine five hundred people in the court of law, each of them taking the stand reporting what they saw." Well said. I can't think of any stronger evidence than the testimony of hundreds of people who saw Him with their own eyes.

And about Jesus' crew of friends Shai says, "The disciples weren't stupid guys who would ruin their lives and choose to die for what they knew was a lie."[2] Those "twelve" that He appeared to eventually went on to lay down their lives for Him. They saw the resurrected Christ and died as His faithful witnesses.

OUR RESPONSE

So there it is. That is the greatest news in all of the universe. I promise you'll never hear a story that comes anywhere close. But how should you respond to it?

There's some news that doesn't affect our lives very much. Maybe we hear a story about the president's approval ratings or we read an article about a new celebrity marriage, but what do those things really matter? We'll likely go on with our lives as if nothing happened.

The good news is not that kind of news. The gospel is the kind of news that changes *everything*. And it's the kind of news that affects everybody. This news demands a response from you. Here's where faith in a good God begins.

REPENT AND BELIEVE

Many people assume that God wants us to do good stuff to earn His acceptance, but that's simply untrue. Our "righteousness" is about as clean as a dirty diaper. Performing for God is the wrong way to respond. We should look away from what we can do, and start looking at what Christ has done. Christ said that those who lose their lives will gain them (Matthew 10:39). My good life begins at the end of me.

The proper response to the good news is faith and repentance. Biblical faith means, first, understanding what the truth is. Do you understand what the gospel says—that Christ died for sinners and rose from the grave? Do you understand that you are helpless and can only be saved by grace through faith? Second, it means agreeing with that truth. Do you accept that these events actually happened and that we can be saved by faith in Christ? And third, it means trusting in those truths. This means relying on the good news about Christ and ordering our lives around Him.

Growing up, I called myself a Christian because I had heard the facts and agreed with them. But looking back, I don't think I really was a Christian because I hadn't truly trusted in Jesus. My life hadn't changed and I still relied solely on myself. I was lacking that third aspect of true faith. Missing that third part is the difference between acknowledging a lifesaving drug and actually taking it. It's the difference between saying "I hear a bomb," and actually getting out of the building. This kind of halfway faith is useless. Faith that doesn't affect your life isn't really faith.

This is where repentance comes in. In Mark 1:15 Jesus says, "repent and believe in the gospel." Repentance means turning away from your sins, and turning to God, and it goes hand in hand with true faith. If you really believe that you've sinned against God and that your sins are so horrible that the only perfect man in history had to die for them—you'd turn away from those sins. If you believed that Jesus was the rightful Lord of your life, you'd gladly end your love affair with sin to follow after Him.

Trusting in Christ means more than asking Him into your heart. It's more than praying a prayer. It means believing on His name and depending on Him for salvation. It means making a commitment to leave your sin behind, and follow Him because you trust Him as Lord.

There is no in-between response to the good news. You either receive it or reject it. You either believe in Christ or reject Him. You either turn from your sin or you cling to it. But this is where the good life begins.

THE RESULT

Our life on this earth is extremely important, but nothing is more important than our forever fate. Those who trust in Christ are given eternal life and will never perish (John 3:16). God's offer of salvation is available to all. "Everyone who calls on the name of the Lord will be saved" (Romans 10:13).

The Lord moved my heart to repent and believe in the good news, and I'm blown away by His grace. We can be treated as if we never sinned. We can be righteous before God! We can be adopted into God's family. We can be indwelled by God's Spirit. We can be empowered to follow Him. We can begin to live the good life.

If you've trusted in the good news, God has made you a brand-new person. He's done it for a reason. You've been redeemed for the glory of God. You were made for God, and He's saved you so that you can honor Him like you were made to. Faith in this good news doesn't only begin the good life; it sustains us until our faith becomes sight. Until then, each of us must live by faith in this good news every single day.

LYRICS FROM "LOVE ON DISPLAY"

There was nothing 'bout me that moved you to love
I was born unclean in a pool of blood
But you said live, you really proved your love
Christ took my death, my noose is loosened up
You saw me full of sin, full of lust, rage
You hated my sin because of all your just ways
But you pitied me, showered me with much grace
I read the Good News printed on the front page
The headline read, "Christ for my lust paid
For my sin died, then He was just raised"
And the way I knew the grace from you was real sweet
Is that you came and died while I was still weak
What compassion you showed
Displayed your great love with action, yeah the facts in the Scroll
Now I'm like a "dirty burlap sack full of gold"
You put treasure in a clay pot, I'm amped to behold[3]

5

THE GOOD BOOK

AFTER I BECAME A CHRISTIAN, God changed my entire world. I began to see everything in a new light. It's like He gave me new spiritual taste buds, because I began to love new things, and hate some of the things I used to love. My growth was very slow at first. I struggled to shake many of the sins I had indulged in before. I even began sinning in areas I hadn't struggled with before. I was a very immature Christian.

But by God's grace, something changed. I started to read God's Word ferociously. I didn't really know much about the Scriptures, except what I remembered from the children's Bible my grandmother gave me as a kid. But when I began to read it seriously, God met me and I started to grow. I remember the first time I read a passage that I was able to apply to a specific situation in my life. It blew me away! Here was the power I needed to sustain and grow my new life.

BREATHE

As I write this chapter, my wife and I are expecting our first son. When he's born, he'll be thrust into a new world where he has to breathe. He's very much alive right now, but his life on this earth will begin when he takes that first breath of oxygen. We'll mark the day he takes that first breath as his birth day.

His life will begin by breathing in oxygen, and every moment that my son lives will be lived by breathing in oxygen. If he is kept away from oxygen for too long, his body will begin to shut down, and eventually his life will end. He needs oxygen.

Well in similar fashion, believers are reborn by the Word of truth. God's Word is the oxygen that He uses to bring us to life. And God's Word is the very same oxygen that we need to continually breathe as we press forward. If we stop taking in God's Word, the consequences are deadly. The good life is sustained by faith in God's Word.

WHAT IS THE GOOD BOOK?

Many people think of the Bible as a man-made book full of mythical stories and bad history. People may get a verse tattooed into their skin, but it never makes it into their hearts. They think the Bible is old school, irrelevant, and dead, so they ignore it. And if they're right, we should ignore it too. We shouldn't waste our time reading strange, old stories or wrestle with the difficult teachings of Jesus. If it's just a book full of men's opinions, then we should just live by our own, or at least some that are more modern. I have no desire to read dead, old books that aren't true. The Bible isn't dead though. It's very much alive.

Those skeptics were right about one thing: the Good Book is old. It's a collection of writings penned over the span of thousands of years. Each of these "books" was written by men "carried along by the Holy Spirit" (2 Peter 1:21). You could say the Holy Spirit was a kind of ghostwriter. God dictated some of it word for word to the authors, but not all of it. Most of the Good Book is written in the words of the authors, but all of the content is the truth of God.

They communicated His truth from their perspective, and God's Spirit guided the process. As 2 Timothy says, "All Scripture is breathed out by God . . ." (2 Timothy 3:16). It's sort of like a dad giving his sons a coloring book, telling them which pages to color, and helping them color inside the lines. God allowed men to do the writing, but He carried them along and didn't allow any falsehood or error. Every word is breathed out by the eternally perfect God of the universe. Because God Himself is trustworthy, we can trust His words. Because the Bible is God's Word, we can build our lives upon it.

THE PURPOSE OF THE GOOD BOOK

We should be deeply grateful to God for revealing Himself in the Word. We take it for granted. What would it be like if God did not reveal Himself to us?

If God didn't reveal Himself to us we would be pretty clueless about Him. We wouldn't know who He is, what He's like, or what He expects from us. He's beyond us and our world. We can't meet Him for lunch or send Him a text message. He has to "come down to our level" and communicate with us in a way we can understand. He's graciously done that in His Word.

Many of us have used our imaginations and created our own personal gods. Almost like a Build-A-Bear or a little girl's doll. We grab the parts we think are necessary, we clothe him with our own ideas, and we make him into a god that we like. Maybe our imaginary god doesn't judge anyone, or maybe he would never allow evil to happen.

I'm sure these imaginary gods make us feel better, but we can't just do that. God is a real being with a real personality and real attributes. God creates man—not the other way around. In order for us to truly know God, He must tell us about Himself.

Also, if God did not reveal Himself to us we would be clueless about life. We would know absolutely nothing for sure. No one would have an authoritative word on anything. What are we here for? What is right and wrong? What happens after this life? Without God's Word, we wouldn't have sure answers for any of those questions. Your guess would be as good as mine—about everything. Expecting man to understand life without God is like expecting an uneducated man to explain astrophysics. How could he possibly know anything about it unless an authority on the subject taught him?

In His Word, God has told us what we're here for. He's given us guidance about right and wrong according to His character. He's given us the good news through which we can receive eternal life. He's given us all the answers we need about life. Any opinions or worldviews that contradict Scripture, are wrong. His Word is the final authority on everything it speaks about.

BREATHING FOR THE RIGHT REASONS

Many people use the Bible incorrectly. They go to the Bible merely to find inspirational stories, or to learn more so they can sound "deep." But in light of what we just discussed, what are the right motivations for going to God's Word?

One, we should go to the Word to meet with God. If we've been restored to God through Christ, we have access to Him. We have a personal relationship with the God of the universe. It would be nice if I woke up every morning and God physically appeared in my room like a magic genie, but that's not how He works. That doesn't mean we can't meet with Him, and even "see" Him.

The beginning of 1 Samuel tells us the story of young Samuel, and chapter 3 says that "God appeared [to Samuel] again at Shiloh . . ." We might think, "Wow Samuel is lucky! I wish God would appear to me sometimes. Then my faith would be stronger." Well look at how God appeared to him, ". . . for the Lord revealed Himself to Samuel at Shiloh by the word of the Lord" (1 Samuel 3:21).

Samuel is not alone. We too can look upon the Lord. We too can meet with God, but not just in a special place like Shiloh. We can meet with Him anywhere. We can read of His works and sit in awe of His glory. We can listen to His comforting words and reflect on His fatherly care for us. Time in the Word isn't like reading a regular book; it's actually spending time with a person. Therefore, we should come to the Word expecting to meet with our Maker.

Two, we should go to the Word to see how to walk out our faith. Scripture tells us how God's people should live. James 1:22 says, "But be doers of the word, and not hearers only, deceiving yourselves." James warns us against deceiving ourselves by thinking that hearing is enough. Hearing alone isn't what pleases God. Hearing must be accompanied by faith and obedience.

One time, about five or six years ago, I was on tour for a few months and I didn't pay close attention to my bank account.

While I had plenty of money in my savings, my checking account had been depleted by a bunch of snacks, magazines, and other purchases on the road. Every time I made a purchase, my bank—or should I say my former bank—charged me thirty dollars to transfer the money from my savings. So for example, instead of paying fifty cents for some lemonheads I bought at the airport, I paid $30.50.

When I returned home and discovered my tragic mistake, I pleaded with a manager at the bank to help me out. After all, I had sufficient money in my savings for all of those purchases. I admit I wasn't rich, but I could definitely afford lemonheads! It didn't matter what I had in my savings though. If it never got applied to the right account, it was irrelevant how much money I had saved up. It's the same thing with hearing God's Word. You can read and read and read. You can listen to a million sermons. You can even go to seminary. But if what you hear never gets applied to your life, it means nothing. If you never actually believe it and obey, your knowledge is worthless. Don't deceive yourself.

Three, we should go there to feed our faith. The good life is lived by faith in a good God. Romans 10:17 says, "Faith comes through hearing and hearing through the word of Christ." Faith is a gift from God, and His Word is where He gives it to us.

Our faith began when we heard the Word, and it is sustained the same way. We took our first spiritual breath by the Word (specifically, the gospel) and God's Word is the air we must continue to breathe for every moment of our spiritual lives.

Our three main enemies—the world, the flesh, and the Devil—still lie to us every single day. They tell us that deceiving someone to get out of a bind is acceptable. They tell us that the pleasures of pornography are worth the havoc it wreaks on our souls. These lies are like a poison that slowly eats away at our faith until we stop believing the truth. They blind us to reality. They suffocate us and suck the life out of us. We need to breathe.

We've been freed from bondage to these lies, but we must keep them from reclaiming the upper hand. We all know how to fight lies—with truth. If we were to discover that false rumors had been spread about us, what would we do? We would try to vindicate our names by telling people what really happened. In everyday life we understand that the only way to fight lies is with the truth.

The same is true of the lies that our enemies tell us. We fight those lies with the truth of God. This is seen most clearly in the story of Jesus' temptation. Satan comes to Jesus and tells Him many lies, attempting to get the Lord to obey him instead of the Father. Yet Jesus fights him off, by the Word of God. He counters every lie with truth from God's Word (Luke 4:1–12). He not only defeats the Enemy for us, but He gives us a model for walking in the victory He purchased for us.

BREATHING TECHNIQUES

How should we take in God's Word?

1. We should read God's Word prayerfully. As we discussed earlier, time in the Good Book is spending time with a person. As we read beautiful things about God we should be responding to Him in prayer. We should be praising Him for His goodness. We should be thanking Him for what He's done for us. We should be pleading with Him to give us faith to believe and obey. We should be asking Him to help us understand what we're reading. After all, God's Word is not magic. It's not like you read a verse and automatically become more holy. God works in us by His Spirit when we read His Word. So we should plead with Him to do that work in our hearts.

2. We should read God's Word humbly. We should come to the Word with the right posture. We should be willing to sit at His feet and hear what He has to say. We should come acknowledging that the Creator of the universe is speaking. We should be ready to rearrange our lives in light of what He says. We should be prepared to surrender our opinions and habits. No words are more important than His.

3. We should read God's Word carefully and studiously. Many people think that "studying" God's Word turns Him into a subject and surrenders true intimacy with Him. I strongly disagree. That would be like me saying, "I love my wife, but I shouldn't listen to her too closely. If I dig deep and ask her what she thinks, I might ruin our relationship." Deep intimacy with God comes when we behold Him and labor to get to know Him in His Word. Our goal should always be discovering what the author was intending to communicate to us about God and His will. We don't want to play the "what this means to me" game. We should strive to arrive at the true meaning, that we would hear what God is saying to us and not just what we want to hear.

Sometimes it's good to spend a few hours on one verse. It's a good thing to look at other resources that help us understand the historical context. If we really want to know God we should be willing to dig deep.

4. We should read God's Word often. I don't know about you, but I have bad spiritual memory. I can be rocked by a passage at eight o'clock in the morning and be rebelling against it by one o'clock in the afternoon. The truth that awakens faith in my heart can easily be forgotten in a matter of hours. I need to be in the Word often!

It's been said that we never drift toward Jesus. Any drift is always a drift away from Him, because our sinful hearts lean toward sin. Every moment I don't cling to the truth of God, I'm being deceived by the lies of the enemy. Our hearts will often buck against the truth, and in those times we need God's Word to put us back in check.

THE WORD AT WORK

When I began to read God's Word diligently, I began to grow quickly. And the more I saw God in His Word, the more I wanted to see Him. Most of us don't read the Word because we've never read the Word. If you only knew the precious gems that await you in the Good Book, you would probably sacrifice some of your time on Facebook.

I talked to a friend recently who told me he hasn't read God's Word in a very long time. To be honest, when he said those words I was afraid for his soul. Not because there's some magic amount of time out of God's Word that leads to hell. And not because I think God can't keep Him. I was afraid because I know that God uses His Word as a means to keep us. If we stop breathing, we won't live. But if we truly believe in Christ we will never stop breathing and taking in His Word.

God's Word is the air we breathe. His Word alone can give me life. His Word alone can sustain my life. His Word is the road map to the good life.

LYRICS FROM "KNOW ME"

(Written as if the Good Book is speaking)

I'm so old school, but I'm relevant to new
In a league of my own, known for telling them the truth
I know some fakes that oppose, but I'm telling 'em to move
Because they ain't on my level, like my elevator moved
They try to hang, and compete with what I bring
But it just ain't the same, they miss, they playing games
I got truth that they missing and power they can't obtain
They fakes, they not real, one day they will be ashamed
No challengers can harm me, I battle in a storm
I know folks that got my quotes tatted on their arms
But they missing the point, from Atlanta to the Bronx
If they lives don't change, and they patterns ain't informed
I give you data, speak on matters that'll form
The way you see the world, from your calories to porn
If you hear me but never change you better be alarmed
I need doers not hearers that's the norm.[1]

6

GOOD PEOPLE

I WAS A YOUNG MAN, excited about Jesus and following hard after Him. I had begun to ferociously study the Bible, and I was rapidly growing. God's Word was real and alive to me, and it showed. But there came a time when I felt like I was hitting the ceiling in my spiritual growth. I couldn't get past certain sins and I didn't know why. But one day, it hit me like a jab from Pacquiao. My growth had been halted because I was trying to walk it out on my own.

It's not that I never talked with other Christians. I attended church services every week, and had Christian friends I would hang out with. But our relationships were very limited. We had a great time together, but our conversations about our spiritual lives were pretty shallow. We weren't exhorting each other in the Word. And I didn't tell them about the sins I was still struggling with.

I was being foolish; almost like the husband who doesn't know where he's going but refuses to ask for directions. God had given me people to help me, but I refused to receive the help. Since then I've learned that the good life is not lived in isolation, but rather in community with "good people."

ADOPTED INTO A FAMILY

Imagine for a second a young boy, living as an orphan, who was adopted by a loving family. They bring him home, feed him, and give him his own room. He loves his new parents, and he's learning how to spell his new last name! But when his new parents introduce him to his new brothers and sisters, he wants nothing to do with them. He's glad to be a part of the family, yet he rejects his brothers and sisters?

All believers have been adopted by God and are now His children. But we often forget that we were adopted into a family of adopted children. We can't take on our Father's name and ignore the rest of the family. We all bear His name. The group of people around the world that bear His name can collectively be called the church.

The church is not a building people meet in on Sundays; the church is the people that meet there. One author defines the church as "the body of people called by God's grace through faith in Christ to glorify him together by serving him in his world."[1] I think that's a good, biblical definition. Anyone who puts their faith in Christ is part of the universal church. Within that larger body of believers around the world, there are local churches as well. This is usually what the New Testament means when it uses the word *church*. But many people don't share the Bible's excitement about this group of people.

MISCONCEPTIONS

The church has been given a bad name. Some of that has been earned by so-called churches that look nothing like Jesus. Some of that has been unfair stereotyping from skeptics. But there's no doubt that the church isn't respected and valued in our day. What do you think of when you hear the word "church"?

A lot of people think of self-righteous hypocrites. Others think of shiny choir robes and screaming preachers. Some may think of boring, long services. And still others probably just think, "Not for me." One rapper even said, and I paraphrase, "If you scared then go to church."[2] As if the church is only a place for frail and timid people.

We need to move beyond those misconceptions. The good life cannot be lived apart from good people. I don't call the church "good people" because the members are perfect, but because they've been purchased by a good God. These are people who are being conformed to the image of their Savior, and are doing good works in God's world. These people have put their faith in a good God, and together they are striving to live by faith.

THE CHURCH IS IMPORTANT BIBLICALLY

It's become popular in our day and age to refer to oneself as "spiritual, but not religious." One of the things that people often mean is that they have a relationship with God, but they don't like church. So they'll pray and maybe even read their Bibles in private, but they don't gather with others to seek God as a community.

That way they can have almighty God without all the drama. They figure they can love God without loving His people. That might sound nice to some, except it's not the picture the Bible paints of Christianity. Biblical Christianity happens in community, and the church is not something insignificant that we can toss to the side like an unwanted nuisance.

In the gospel of Matthew, Peter confesses that Jesus is "the Christ the Son of the living God" (Matthew 16:16). Immediately following that confession, Jesus told Peter that He would build His church and that "the gates of hell shall not prevail against it" (Matthew 16:18b). Jesus planned to build an organism so strong that nothing could stop it. Ephesians 5 compares the church to a bride, saying, "Christ loved the church and gave himself up for her" (Ephesians 5:25). Jesus laid His life down for the church, so clearly it was important to Him.

All but one of Paul's New Testament letters were written to either churches or church leaders. This is because he doesn't have a context for Christians doing life apart from other Christians. The assumption was that Christians would follow Christ together, as they always had. The book of Acts tells us about the first Christians and the way they lived life together. Acts 2 says, "They devoted themselves to the apostles' teaching and the fellowship, to the breaking of bread and the prayers" (Acts 2:42).

The entire New Testament talks about following Jesus in the context of community. This altogether private Christianity that many people pursue doesn't exist in the Bible. Anyone who calls themselves a Christian does not have the right to discard the church as if it's optional.

COLLECTIVE MISSION

Christians are those whom God has saved by His grace. And He's given us the privilege of joining Him in His work in the world. In the gospels Jesus says that we are to be the light of the world and the salt of the earth. We should be shining light in our dark communities, and showing the world a picture of what Jesus looks like. Think about how powerful it is to see an individual whose life has been changed by the gospel of Jesus

Christ. Now think about how much more powerful it would be to see a whole community of such individuals, a community of young and old, black and white, rich and poor. It shows onlookers the power of the gospel that's available to all.

At the center of the work God has given the church is the duty to proclaim the very same good news that saved us. The commission Jesus gave us was to "Go therefore and make disciples of all nations, baptizing them in the name of the Father and of the Son and of the Holy Spirit, teaching them to observe all that I have commanded you" (Matthew 28:19–20). Family, we have work to do.

A Christian ignoring God's people is like a soldier ignoring the rest of the troops and trying to defeat the enemy's army by himself. That's not how it works! There's a whole army for a reason—they need each other to win. Our General has given us a mission in the world, and we must carry it out as a unit.

STAY CLOSE

Animals are smarter than you think. Many species travel in packs as opposed to traveling alone. They have an instinct within them that tells them to stay close to the pack, otherwise they won't be able to survive. The pack helps to protect them from attackers. They hunt as a team instead of individually. They understand that they need the pack in order to live. Believers would stay close to the pack if they understood that they needed the pack to survive.

The truth is, each of us is weak. We've been saved and we've been given new hearts, but we are prone to stray. We are prone to ignore God's Word and to resist His Spirit. We are prone to once again believe lies fed to us by the world, the flesh, and the Devil. We desperately need other believers in our lives to remind us of the truth.

Anybody who's been a Christian for more than five minutes will tell you that following Jesus is hard. Even those of us with the most rock-solid confidence in Christ have moments when our faith weakens and our obedience wanes. We have moments of insanity, and we need our brothers and sisters to talk some sense into us.

The church should be a community where the Word is passed and echoed from person to person continually. God has actually given other Christians gifts for the sake of building you up. A good church knows that only God's Word can sustain life and awaken faith, therefore the Word stays central.

STOP HIDING

All this community talk is frightening for some of us. It scares us because all that "spiritual, but not religious" talk is really just an excuse to hide. We don't want to do life with other Christians because we don't want them to see what we're really like. It's easier to look like we have it all together from afar. Sadly, some of us are more concerned with looking Christlike, than doing what it takes to actually become Christlike.

Others of us know that once we have other Christians in our lives, we'll have to answer to others about our sin, and eventually we'll have to repent. Isolation seems like the safest place to be, when in reality there is nowhere more dangerous. Satan often uses isolation to lure us away from Christ. He wants to get us away from the pack so he can attack us when we are defenseless, with no one to help. So open your life up to others. They have a right—better yet a command—to be in your life.

TOUR GUIDES

When I first began to follow Jesus, I saw commands in God's Word, but didn't know what they looked like practically. So for example, I knew that I was supposed to work out my salvation "with fear and trembling" (Philippians 2:12b). I knew that one day I would be called to love my wife "as Christ loved the church" (Ephesians 5:25). But I didn't know what those things looked like practically. So what happened? God graciously sent men into my life who loved Jesus and modeled it for me. If it hadn't been for these men, I don't know where I'd be.

I didn't consider these men to be my Lord, or the authority on everything. I didn't follow them in the ways that they strayed from Christ. But I followed them as they followed Him. They taught me how to follow Christ well, almost like a tour guide. They didn't create the way, but they helped me follow the path. We're brothers in pursuit of the same goal, but they showed me the trail they took. I'm grateful for those men. Use mature believers as your spiritual tour guides.

DIE TO YOU

For much of this chapter, we've talked about how "good people" help you to live the good life. But in case you didn't already know, it's not all about you. God has given gifts to other believers so they can build you up, but He's also given you gifts so you can build them up.

So you should be looking to discover what gifts you've been given and you should use them to build others up. You should be exhorting others with the Word. And you should be holding others accountable. You should be looking to be a spiritual tour guide for others. You are part of a family, and you have responsibilities to help keep the family strong.

I know many of us have never seen a healthy church. Others of us have been hurt by the church. And I know there are even some of us who just don't care for the church. But God knows what's best for us. He saved us so that we can live the good life, and He's given us others to help us.

I encourage you to find a church that looks like what we've talked about. One that preaches the gospel, one that centers on Christ and His Word, and one that welcomes all that will turn away from their sin. Trying to find this kind of church can be hard, but it's not optional for us. We can ignore man's ideas, but we can't ignore God's. Take heed to the Bible's picture of Christianity, lest you create your own religion. Commit yourself to others, both for their benefit and your own.

In the beginning of this chapter, I reflected on my own journey. I struggled to grow because I ignored one of the main places where God gives me grace. But once I really opened up and allowed others into my life I began to grow rapidly again. When I think back, all of the significant seasons of growth in my life were in some way tied to walking with other believers. God used His people to make a big difference in my life. They helped me to walk by faith.

Don't ignore one of the main places where God gives you grace. Walk with good people.

LYRICS FROM "GOOD PEOPLE"

Good people, you might wonder why I call them that
Is it 'cause they're perfect? Nah, but He bought them back
They're like no one else I've ever seen
Pick the prettiest painting, still they're a better scene
They're all over the world, they were hellish fiends
But they changed and now they follow a jealous King
They're renewed, remade—He saves
He made a purchase and gave them new b-days
Now they try to mimic all the King's ways
Folks watch them like, "I've seen this before, it's like a replay"
They're still weak, so on His Word they stand
Fear and trembling—they call that their workout plan
Body builders, yeah they take a verse out man
And they spot one another, 'cause they got one another
You're a means of grace, when I'm running in place
We're His bride, I need y'all for running this race
You're good people.[3]

SECTION III:

HOW DO I LIVE THE GOOD LIFE?

7

GOOD **WORKS**

"YOU'RE NOT THE BOSS OF ME!" Surely we've all heard that phrase before. Since our childhoods, we all have something inside of us that really values freedom. We want to be our own bosses. We don't want to allow anybody to tell us what to do or how we should behave. That way of thinking drives the way we live our lives. Many of us think of the good life as a life free from any boundaries.

Recently I read about a celebrity who unashamedly carries porn with him wherever he goes. He doesn't hide it or deny it. Why should he be ashamed? He's not doing anything illegal and he enjoys looking at it. That seems to be his whole thought process on morality. Is it legal? Do I like it? Am I a grown man? Then I can do it.

In this picture of the good life you're free to do whatever you please. And if anyone—even God—tries to intrude on your "freedom," you should just respond with an uncompromising, "You're not the boss of me!"

TRUE FREEDOM

But real freedom is not the freedom to do whatever you feel like. Nobody would want that kind of freedom for a young boy who feels like playing in a busy street. That sort of freedom is dangerous. True freedom is being freed up to live the way you were created to live. We want freedom from evil tyranny, not freedom from loving leadership.

Our sinful hearts are cruel dictators. And as long as they rule over us, we're not free. We're robots. But when we begin to follow the loving leadership of our Father in Heaven, we'll begin to experience true liberty.

I know a twenty-one-year-old man who refuses to get drunk and sleep around like the rest of the brothers in his fraternity. I know a fifty-year-old woman who opened a pregnancy center to serve young women in her community. I know a family that doesn't even own a TV because they don't want to waste too much time sitting on the couch. What would drive these people to order their lives this way? Surely that's not what they always feel like doing. These people are driven by their faith in a good God to do good works. What kinds of works are you driven to?

When I use the word "works" I basically mean our actions. I'm talking about everything we do and say. Every moment of every day we will be faced with choices—moral forks in the road. We'll be placed in our own "Garden of Eden" and we'll be given the same test Adam and Eve were given. There's only one question on this exam: will you believe and obey God, or believe and obey the Enemy? The good life is the life spent believing God, and our works will always reflect whether or not we're taking Him at His Word.

WALK IT OUT

Every now and then, some rapper with a bulletproof vest and menacing album cover will have his personal life exposed. He raps about shooting dudes, but in reality the only time he shoots people is with his iPhone camera. And when the truth comes out, the whole world sees that he's not so gangsta after all. This can be fatally damaging to a rapper's career. You lose credibility when your lifestyle doesn't match up with what you say.

While I would never want to encourage anyone to live a violent lifestyle, I do think our lives have to match up with who we claim to be. Even pop culture recognizes that we should expect a certain kind of behavior from certain kinds of people. Babies cry, politicians self-advertise, and gangstas—well, they do gangsta stuff. What kind of behavior should we expect from those who are living by faith in a good God? What kind of works should mark those who are living the good life?

I think Paul answers that question in Titus chapter 2. He points out two reasons for the death of Jesus. He says, "[Jesus] gave himself for us to redeem us from all lawlessness and to purify for himself a people for his own possession who are zealous for good works" (Titus 2:14). God sent His Son to die, in part, so that we would be a people "zealous" for good works. Not just open to good works, but passionately pursuing them. Zeal for good works is what happens when we believe the good news. We become brand-new people, and that should always show up in our actions.

BE WHO YOU ARE

What would you think if you saw two parents walking down the street being ordered around by their two-year-old? Imagine the toddler screaming, "I don't care what you want, we're going to the circus! Cancel your meetings and take me!" The parents then respond, "Yes sir, whatever you want, son."

At first you would probably be caught off guard at such an intelligent, yet mean two-year-old. But then you would wonder, "Why do they let him tell them what to do? Don't they know that they're the parents?" And you would be right. That mother and father don't have to do what their son says. It would be strange to see parents yielding to the demands of their toddler.

It's just as strange to see believers yielding to the demands of conquered sin. The apostle Paul wrestles with this tension in Romans 6. "How can we who died to sin still live in it?... We know that our old self was crucified with him in order that the body of sin might be brought to nothing, so that we would no longer be enslaved to sin" (Romans 6:2,6).

When Jesus died on the cross, He stood toe-to-toe with our sin and dealt it a death blow. And when we put our faith in Christ, Jesus severed the sin-shackles that kept us bound. We're free! So it would be insane for us to go on sinning. When we continue to live in sin, we are insisting on return-ing to slavery. We are clinging to a cruel master who hates us. Instead of walking in our old ways, we are to "walk in newness of life" (Romans 6:4b).

First Peter 1:14–15 says, "As obedient children, do not be conformed to the passions of your former ignorance, but as he who called you is holy, you also be holy in all your con-duct." Yet, in chapter 2, Peter says that we are already "a holy nation" (1 Peter 2:9). God has already set us apart as a holy people for His use and He sees us through the lens of His holy Son. In that sense, we are already holy!

So the battle for the believer is not trying to change who we are, Jesus has already done that. We are new creations

(2 Corinthians 5:17). Our battle is to live in light of our new identity. Our battle is to walk in the victory that Jesus won on our behalf. When we sin, we are reverting back to the old us. But when we're holy in our conduct, we're reflecting our new identity.

Colossians 3 talks about putting off our earthly works and putting on new ones. The earthly works are the sinful deeds Jesus died for, and the new ones are the Christlike qualities God works in us by His Spirit.

We've been drafted by God and now we're on His team. Therefore as believers, we have to take off our old uniforms (earthly deeds), and put on our new ones (good works). It's not a one-time thing though. It's an everyday thing. We will continue to mess up, but we have to repent and trust in Christ anew. The Christian life is marked by daily repentance and faith in God.

WORKS OF LOVE

So what are these good works supposed to look like? The Good Book is always going to be our guide for living the way we were created to live. Throughout the Scriptures, we see an abundance of commands about what our lives should look like. All of these commands are a reflection of God's perfect character.

It would be seemingly impossible to summarize these

commands in one chapter—yet Jesus did it in about four sen-
tences. In the gospel of Matthew, a lawyer questioned Jesus
and asked Him what the greatest commandment was. First
Jesus said, "You shall love the Lord your God with all your
heart and with all your soul and with all your mind. This is the
great and first commandment" (Matthew 22:37–38).

Jesus is basically saying that we should love God with all of
our being and energy. Our love for God should be far greater
than our love for anything else. And this love for God should
show up in our decisions, our jobs, and the way we use our
time. All of our works should be marked by a love for God.

But Jesus didn't stop with that commandment. Next He
said, "And a second is like it: You shall love your neighbor as
yourself" (Matthew 22:39). Our love for God should lead us to
love those whom He created. So we can no longer afford to be
self-centered. We can no longer just look out for ourselves;
we should, with the same vigor, look out for others. We should
be actively seeking the good of all people—even our enemies!

The Bible's radical teaching on loving others seems strange
to some. During the Civil Rights Movement, Christians were
criticized by leaders like Malcolm X for loving the very people
that hated them. It seems strange to seek the good of those
who seek your demise. But this is the radical change Jesus
works in the hearts of His people. Seeking the good of others
is what happens when you follow a Savior who laid down His

life to seek our good.

Who are your enemies? Have you been intentionally reaching out to them in love? If not, you're missing a precious opportunity to show them the love of Christ. Have you intentionally loved on your family members? The people in your neighborhood? A lack of love for others should make us question our love for God. If you love Him, then love them.

Love is often used as a way to summarize good works in the Scriptures. All of our works must be characterized by love.

THE PURPOSE OF GOOD WORKS

If you're like me, sometimes you do good things, hoping other people see them. You may not tell people all the good things you're doing, but you sure hope they notice. You want them to think to themselves, "Wow, I can't believe they did that! What a great person." But that's not God's purpose for calling us to do good works.

We have not been called to labor for our own glory, but for God's. Jesus tells His disciples, " . . . let your light shine before others, so that they may see your good works and give glory to your Father who is in heaven" (Matthew 5:16). God doesn't want us to do good works so that people will say, "Wow, what a nice guy." God wants His people to do good works, so that people will say, "Wow, what a great God!" and "Who is this God who transforms lives and works through His people?" Our good works can accomplish many good things in the world, but none of these are more important than the glory of God.

MOTIVATED BY FAITH

We often think that God is only concerned with what we do. But just as important as what we do is why we do it. We don't do good works in order to earn God's favor or save ourselves. That's an insult to God and a denial of the good news. We do good works because God has already saved us. It is an outworking of our faith.

Hebrews 11:6 says, "Without faith it is impossible to please God" (NIV). Our faith in Christ must be the driving force behind our good works. If it weren't for God's Spirit, we wouldn't be able to do any good works. We should plead with Him to work faith-filled good works in our lives.

So by all means, serve at your local soup kitchen. By all means, read your Bible every day. By all means, serve your spouse by doing the dishes. But strive to do those good works from a heart of faith.

THE GOOD WORKS OF JESUS

Still, after all this good works talk, some of us may be confused. What do these good works actually look like in action? Look no further than the Lord Jesus Christ. He didn't struggle with evil works like you and me. Jesus said, "I always do the things that are pleasing to him" (John 8:29). He lived in perfect obedience for His entire earthly life. Unlike other men, Jesus has no flaws or moral weaknesses. We can safely model our every move after Him—His decision making, His speech, His love, His everything. Jesus lived the good life and showed us what it means to obey God by faith.

We can learn just as much from His death as we can from His life. If you read the New Testament, you'll see that the cross is the greatest picture of all Christian virtues. Philippians 2 points to the death of Christ as the perfect example of humility. Hebrews 12 points to the death of Christ as the perfect example of endurance. 1 John 3:16 points to the death of Jesus as the perfect example of love. I could go on and on. The moral of this story is look to Christ!

Look to Christ as the one who did good works. Look to Christ as the one who died so that we would do good works. Look to Christ as the one who forgives us when we fail to do good works. And look to Christ as the one who, by His Spirit, enables us to do good works.

If you're a Christian, you've been redeemed by His sacrifice and you are now a new creation. Your sins are covered, and you've been freed to follow hard after Jesus. Sin is no longer your master! Believe it and live like it.

LYRICS FROM "ROBOT"

Now I've been remade, and I'm no longer hollow
A real Man came, changed everything that I know
He gave me truth, that's a hard pill to swallow
He gave me new commands and He freed me up to follow

Why you always trying to control me?
You are not my boss that's the old me
Obviously, you don't know my style
I'm not a, I'm not a robot now

I am not a robot, I am not a clone
You are not my puppeteer and I am not a drone
I got a new Master and I follow Him alone
I want a good life till I'm gone, it's on

Hey world, you know I see your game
And I don't need your lies, I ain't worried 'bout a thing
Hey devil, I know you want me chained
But you have been defeated, and your power has been drained
Hey flesh, I know you bear my name
I know you love the lies, but I'm steady tryna change
You mighta been confused, but this a new day
I'm saved now, I ain't gotta do what you say!
To my friends, who are still on lockdown
And still controlled by their passions—stop now
'Cause He can free everybody from the top down
If you're freed up, say this with me right now.[1]

8

GOOD STUFF

ONE DAY, EARLIER THIS YEAR, I was staying in the outskirts of Chicago and I needed to take a cab into the city. A yellow taxi pulled up to the hotel and I hopped in the back. Traffic was pretty bad so I had about an hour-long conversation with the driver. His accent tipped me off that he wasn't from Chicago, so I asked him where he was from and how he ended up there.

He said he was from Greece, and that he came to the United States to follow the American dream. I found that pretty interesting so I stopped him and asked, "Did you find it?"

He answered, "I actually did find it. I built my life around money and I eventually became a millionaire." In any other situation I would have given him the twisted up, "C'mon son, I don't believe you" face. But he had been brutally honest our whole conversation and had no reason to lie to me.

As he told me his story, I learned that he had acquired millions, but lost it all when he got greedy. He was trying to make more of the money he loved, but instead he slowly watched his bank account shrink until it was all gone. The very dream that he built his entire life around had been snatched from him in a moment. American dream? Sounds more like a nightmare to me.

LIES

We've been told by our culture that the most important thing in life is the stuff we can acquire. A lot of people point the finger at hip-hop—but hip-hop isn't the source of the problem. American culture is dripping with staunch materialism. Rappers are just bolder and more in your face about it. Wu Tang said cash rules everything around us. Diddy said it was all about the Benjamins. Drake said only broke dudes act like money isn't everything. Hip-hop has been glorifying materialism for years, but the artists learned it from the culture at large.

The rest of our culture pushes the exact same message in a more subtle fashion. Celebrities floss, D-boys hustle, businessmen plot—all in the name of getting more stuff. We've bought into the lie that we are what we have, so we spend our lives chasing it. Rich people love their stuff so they chase after more. Poor people feel like they don't have any stuff so they spend their lives trying to get some. But is this really what the good life is all about? Those who are living the good life use stuff; they don't worship it.

WEALTH IS FUTILE

We've been trained to build our lives around things that don't last. A lot of people say, "Life is short, so get everything you can while you can." They think that's living it up, but it doesn't seem very wise to me. That's almost like saying, "This house is eventually going to burn down, so stash as much stuff there as you possibly can." Huh? Why spend all my energy hoarding something that will eventually burn? "Life is short" makes me want to do the opposite. It makes me want to spend my short life on something that will last long.

In Luke 12:13–21, Jesus tells a parable about a rich man that makes a similar point. The rich man builds a bunch of barns, stores all of his goods, and relaxes. But soon he will die, and someone else will get all of his possessions. Jesus basically calls that man a fool.

It's foolish to spend life acquiring possessions, when our days can end in a moment without warning. And when they do, none of our stuff will matter. First Timothy 6:7 reminds us that "we brought nothing into the world, and we cannot take anything out of the world." We came here empty-handed and we'll leave the same way. We may have had a few things loaned to us, but we won't be able to hold onto them when we die. We should build our lives around things that matter forever.

WEALTH DOESN'T SATISFY

A lot of people would probably object that chasing wealth is worth it, even if it doesn't last, because of the satisfaction it brings us now. But the truth is it doesn't really satisfy. Solomon was a king of Israel, and probably the wealthiest man in the history of the world. His "stuff" would make our stuff look like dirt. He's been there and done that, so I trust his wisdom on the matter. He said, "He who loves money will not be satisfied with money, nor he who loves wealth with his income; this also is vanity" (Ecclesiastes 5:10).

Have you ever noticed that many of the richest people in the world seem to spend their lives . . . trying to get richer? They have what everybody else wants, yet they still want more. Their hearts long for more and more wealth because they aren't truly satisfied. Even with normal folks like you and I, the allure of new shiny cars or gadgets wears off pretty quickly. Our hearts were meant to be satisfied by something greater, but we'll talk more about that later.

DANGEROUS LOVE AFFAIRS

The Scriptures are clear that chasing money not only leaves us unsatisfied, but it also leads us down an ugly path.

Paul exhorts Timothy, saying, "The love of money is a root of all kinds of evils. It is through this craving that some have wandered away from the faith and pierced themselves with many pangs" (1 Timothy 6:10).

It's impossible to have an innocent love affair with money. There's no harmless way to be obsessed with greenbacks. The love of money is like a self-inflicted wound. Building your life around wealth is like shooting yourself in the foot. It's a bad idea.

Money has a way of seducing us and leading us away from God. When we begin to set our eyes on wealth, everything else gets fuzzy. We become blind to everything that really matters, including God. Having a bunch of stuff makes us think all of our needs are met. But money can't take care of all our needs. Only God can meet each and every need. Sometimes the most gracious thing the Lord can do is strip us of our riches, that our attention would be turned back to Him. That's what I pray God was doing with that cab driver I talked about earlier.

Don't misunderstand me though. My goal isn't to demonize money or the stuff money can buy. Material things are not evil. As a matter of fact we should be thankful for the resources we've been given. The Bible is clear that money is not what's gone wrong with the world: sin is. Wealth itself is not a problem. The problem is that sinful people like you and I fall in love with wealth. We think that if we could just have more money, everything would be ok. Let's rethink our perspective on our stuff.

GOD OWNS IT ALL

God owns everything. He bluntly reminds His people of this truth in Psalm 50. He says, with a bit of righteous swagger, "If I were hungry, I would not tell you, for the world and its fullness are mine" (Psalm 50:12). This is important for us to remember, because it will help us grasp the fact that even "our stuff" isn't really our stuff.

When I was a kid, I used to get irritated at my dad for going in my room while I wasn't home. I would say something like, "Come on, Dad! Can you let me have some privacy? That's my room!" He would usually shake his head and reply, "Boy, that's my room. I just let you live in it." I hated when he said that.

The truth is, God could say the exact same thing to every one of us. You may pay rent to your landlord, but God owns that house. Your name may be on your car title, but God owns that vehicle. You may sign at the bottom of your checks, but every penny in that account belongs to God. This is not to say that God doesn't reward hard work, but He definitely doesn't surrender His ownership to any human being.

So should we just stop paying our bills and taking care of our stuff? Absolutely not. We just need to recognize the role we've been given.

MERE MANAGERS

We should think of ourselves as managers instead of owners. God owns everything, but He graciously gives gifts to everybody—believers and nonbelievers. We've been entrusted with a certain amount of stuff that we must manage well as long as we have it.

Imagine that you're starting a new job working for a video company. The boss gives you a million dollars and tells you to use that money to get the best footage possible. A good employee would use that money to buy video equipment, hire people to work on set, etc. A bad employee would use that money for a vacation or other things that have absolutely nothing to do with the mission.

God is our "boss." He's given us resources that we should enjoy, but they are ultimately for His glory. The question is: how well are we managing those resources? Are we seeking His glory or only our enjoyment? Are we thinking strategically about how to spend?

I recently had a conversation with a friend about money. I asked him why he was making a particular purchase, and he said, "I have the money, and I want it, so I'm getting it." That sentence pretty much sums up the way I used to think about money. I didn't make a budget and I didn't think deeply about how I spent my money. I basically just looked to see if I had enough cash in my account. It made plain sense to me.

But Paul gives much stricter guidelines for money in 1 Timothy. He says, "As for the rich in this present age, charge them not to be haughty, nor to set their hopes on the uncertainty of riches, but on God, who richly provides us with everything to enjoy. They are to do good, to be rich in good works, to be generous and ready to share, thus storing up treasure for themselves as a good foundation for the future, so that they may take hold of that which is truly life" (1 Timothy 6:17–19).

MANAGING WELL

Paul gives us a picture here of what it looks like to be a good manager. He clearly doesn't condemn being wealthy. He points to God as the gracious provider. And He gives instructions for how the wealthy should use their wealth. They should use it for good works. Even if we don't consider ourselves wealthy, we should do the same.

Our stuff is not about us. God does want us to enjoy our stuff, but it should never lead to us putting our hope in riches. It should be used for the glory of the one great hope, Jesus Christ.

But what does this look like? Does this mean every dollar should go to missions? No, it doesn't. We should feed ourselves, and provide for our families if we have them. We should pay our bills. It's good to have homes and use those homes to be hospitable. We should give generously to our churches and to the poor. We should freely share our belongings with others in need, especially other believers.

And yes, we should give money to missions. As individuals and churches, we should financially support those who take the message of the good news to others. I can't think of an investment that would yield better return.

Our stuff should be a means to an end and not the end in itself. We don't have stuff for the sake of stuff. We have stuff for the sake of God. We should use our resources for the good works we talked about in chapter seven.

In the 1 Timothy passage above, Paul says that those who refuse to love money in this life, store up treasures for the next one. That teaching sounds a lot like what Jesus says in His most well-known sermon. He says, "Do not lay up for yourselves treasures on earth, where moth and rust destroy and where thieves break in and steal, but lay up for yourselves treasures in heaven, where neither moth nor rust destroys and where thieves do not break in and steal. For where your treasure is, there your heart will be also" (Matthew 6:19–21).

The treasures that we store up on this Earth will eventually fall apart or pass away. But if we would instead use our wealth for good works, God will reward us in glory with everlasting treasure. Yet many of us will still go the way of the rich, young ruler. Choosing earthly treasures over treasures in heaven is like choosing Monopoly money over real currency. Monopoly money is no good in the real world, and earthly treasures are no good in glory. We should strive to store up the eternal instead of the temporal.

Don't believe those preachers who say God's will for your life is that you have all the stuff you want. You won't find anything like that in the Scriptures. Most of the time, when the New Testament talks about wealth, God isn't encouraging us to desire and pursue it. God is warning us about the dangers of pursuing it. Money isn't evil, but we should handle it with caution and guard our hearts.

STRENGTHENED TO DO ALL THINGS

The apostle Paul gives us a beautiful picture of how to relate to our possessions. Once again he doesn't condemn riches, but he also doesn't chase after wealth. Instead he's content. "Not that I am speaking of being in need, for I have learned in whatever situation I am to be content. I know how to be brought low, and I know how to abound. In any and every circumstance, I have learned the secret of facing plenty and hunger, abundance and need. I can do all things through him who strengthens me" (Philippians 4:11–13).

God has strengthened him and given him unwavering contentment. Paul can be content, no matter what circumstances he's in. What about you? Most of us haven't reached this place yet. This kind of contentment only comes once we've set our hope on the Provider and not in the amount of stuff He provides. We should pray that God would strengthen us by His Spirit, and give us this kind of contentment. The good life does not depend on how much stuff we can acquire. The good life depends on a good God.

THE GENEROUS KING

The Lord Jesus is the perfect picture of contentment. You would think that if the Son of God became a man, He would at least be a rich man. Nope. The Scriptures give us clues that suggest He came from a poor family. And as an adult, Jesus Himself said, "Foxes have holes, and birds of the air have nests, but the Son of Man has nowhere to lay his head" (Luke 9:58).

Jesus didn't spend His time acquiring wealth and furnishing His mansion. He didn't even have a home. Instead Jesus spent His time loving others, through teaching, healing, and serving. We should pray for grace to follow His example. This is not to say that none of us should have homes, but that we shouldn't place our hope in those things.

If we ever get to a place where we are hesitant to be generous, we should look to this Lord who's perfectly modeled that as well. Listen to how Paul motivates us to give: "For you know the grace of our Lord Jesus Christ, that though he was rich, yet for your sake he became poor, so that you by his poverty might become rich" (2 Corinthians 8:9).

Though Jesus is the Lord who owns all things, He became a man like you and me. He surrendered His divine wealth, and put on human flesh. He died on the cross and rose from the grave. And He did it for sinners. He traded places with poor rebels so that we could enjoy "unsearchable riches." That's good news (Ephesians 3:8). Our faith in that good news should move us to look more like Him in our own contentment and generosity.

LYRICS FROM "HEART PROBLEM"

Let me get this off my chest
I know some folks gon' be mad
And I ain't trying to start no mess
But I know how folks gon' react
But still I gotta strive and press
And tell them what I mean till they see that
They think I got a problem with dollars and making green cash
But money really ain't the problem
Every grand is a grant from the Father
When I said we can't serve both God and cash, many folk thought I
meant don't bother
But I ain't saying making money ain't right
I'm just saying that your money ain't Christ
So please don't bow down to them greenbacks, and let them
stacks rule your life
I ain't tryna say that we shouldn't get paper
Ain't trying to say that we should stay broke
But money don't mean you got favor
And being broke don't mean that you don't
Money is a gift that's good
Given to give honor to the Giver
I been misunderstood
But I trust in the God who delivers[1]

9

GOOD **DREAMS**

WHEN I WAS A LITTLE KID, I wanted to be a professional baseball player. I would watch Texas Rangers games on TV and I wanted to play for them when I grew up. But then when I got a little older, I wanted to be a basketball player. I dreamed of being a true point guard like Jason Kidd. But then as I got even older, I wanted to be a rapper (maybe because I wasn't that good at baseball or basketball). I loved the way my favorite MCs rocked the mic and I wanted to sell out arenas like them. That seemed like the good life to me. What did you dream about as a kid?

All of us had dreams about what we wanted our lives to look like. Is it possible that some of those dreams were misdirected? Often we dream about what we want to be, and what we hope to accomplish, but only for the sake of being the best us. We just want to be all that we can be.

I want to challenge the way we usually think about dreams and success. I want you to keep dreaming big, but to do so in line with God's will. I want you to dream big by faith.

SUCCESS

Our dreams are usually shaped by what we think is the best, most fulfilling way to spend our time in this world. We don't want to be failures. We only get one life and we want to use it well. So we dream about the kind of success we desire, and we eventually pursue those dreams. But does God see success the same way we do? If we're going to live by faith in a good God, we have to rethink our culture's ideas about "success" and shape our goals around His.

Many of us think of success as "being important," or maybe being at the top of whatever field we work in. We would likely say that the CEO of a company is successful, but we might not say the same about his secretary. We would think of a famous athlete as successful, but we might not say the same of a middle school basketball coach. This is how we define success because these are the goals our culture has put before us. But the truth is, God hasn't commanded us to become CEOs or famous athletes. He hasn't called us to worldly success; He's called us to faithfulness. We need to adjust our goals, and further, adjust our dreams.

CHASING FAITHFULNESS

Have you ever seen those parents that pressure their kids to walk a certain path? Maybe they want them to be a doctor or a lawyer. Others want them to be the athlete or musician they themselves never could be. So they stay in their kids' faces about school. They force them to practice for long hours. And in the most extreme cases, parents shun their children when they don't meet their expectations. They see them as failures.

Well we shouldn't think of our Heavenly Father that way. He's not insisting that His children be at the top of every company, and be the most well known in every field. Instead, He's called us to grind and be faithful wherever we find ourselves.

God doesn't condemn those in "regular" jobs. Instead He calls all of us to "work heartily" (Colossians 3:23). And about those who are idle, Paul says, "Such persons we command and encourage in the Lord Jesus Christ to do their work quietly and to earn their own living" (2 Thessalonians 3:12). In this regard, the business owner and the janitor are on the same playing field. Work hard, do your job well, and do it unto the glory of God.

Often we make the mistake of judging our lives based on the success of others. But that's never helpful. I've always loved the quote, "If God has called you to be a servant, don't stoop so low as to be a king." In God's perspective, higher status does not equal higher value. In fact, God delights in using the weak things of the world "to shame the strong" (1 Corinthians 1:27).

The world puts weight on things that the Lord doesn't. We should strive for greatness, but not according to the world's standards. You should strive to be what God called you to be, not what the world has called you to be. Let faithfulness be the goal that you'll pursue at all costs.

WHOSE GLORY?

If your dream is to be a doctor, that's fine. If your dream is to work at the Apple store, that's fine. If your dream is to be a writer, that's fine. My question for you is: why?

Some of us build our dreams around the ways we can get the most glory for ourselves. We want to be known as the best or the brightest. We want the status that comes along with success. But we must remember that we were not created for our own glory. We were created for the glory of God. Our dreams can't be driven by a desire to be famous. They have to be driven by a desire to glorify God.

When Paul calls us in Colossians 3 to work heartily, he also gives us some motivation for that. He says, "From the Lord you will receive the inheritance as your reward. You are serving the Lord Christ" (Colossians 3:24). We should be working hard, but not for pats on the back from other people. We are servants of Christ and our reward comes from Him.

As believers, God has given us new goals and new passions. We no longer think only about ourselves. We want the lost to hear the gospel. We want to see suffering alleviated. We want the hungry to be fed. We want our God to be glorified. Our dreams have to be built around the passions of God in His Word.

If you're not dreaming big, why not? Where are the believers who dream of running community centers to show Christlike love to their city? Or who dream of serving the needy overseas? Where are the believers who dream of leading a company in a God-honoring way? Where are the believers who dream of being rappers so they can be lights in a dark culture? Those are the kinds of dreams we need.

That's not to say that we should ignore our passions, but that we should use those passions for God's glory. We shouldn't use those passions to make as much money as possible, but to magnify God as much as possible. Our passions must be reshaped around His. We should dream for God's glory.

OPEN HAND

Our culture teaches us that we can do whatever we want if we just put our minds to it. They say if you work hard enough, you will achieve it. But that's not biblically true. Listen to what the psalmist says, "Unless the Lord builds the house, those who build it labor in vain" (Psalm 127:1). Some of us will work harder than everyone else and never reach those "dreams." Unless God blesses our efforts, our work will not succeed.

In a similar vein, some preachers will tell you that if you obey God, He will bring all of your wildest dreams to pass. They say to plan big, follow God, and watch Him give you everything you ever dreamed of. That's simply not true. Proverbs 16:1 says, "The plans of the heart belong to man, but the answer of the tongue is from the Lord." Not every dream is from God, and He doesn't owe it to us to make any of them happen. We should dream big for His glory, and plead with Him to bring those dreams to pass.

But when God doesn't answer our prayers, we shouldn't assume He's unfaithful. We should trust His wisdom. He's far wiser than us and He has already prepared good works for us. We should trust that what He has in store will bring more good to us, and more glory to Him.

The Lord is the final decider for all of our paths. We may operate in different fields, but all of us have the same purpose: to glorify God. That's what we should pursue above all else.

LIVING MY DREAM

For the last ten years, I've dedicated much of my time to making albums and doing concerts. And by God's grace, I've been able to travel the world and make a living doing it. But throughout my career, I've refused to write rhymes that dishonor God. I will not glorify violence, degrade women, or lie about God in my rhymes. Because I've taken that stand, it significantly changes the way the industry receives me.

I could probably be more "successful" if I rapped about the stuff that everybody wants to hear. But my primary goal is not going platinum. My main goal is glorifying God with the gift He's given me. He's given me a gift to honor Him, and a weapon to shoot down faulty worldviews. How could I ever even think about turning and using that weapon on Him? He's given me this gift for His sake, and I choose faithfulness over worldly success.

One day, I'll step away from music because I want to be a pastor. I'm no prophet, but I already know people will call me crazy. They'll say, "But you're still popular and you can still get bigger!" I have bigger dreams than being popular. I want to be faithful. When God calls, I want to answer. That's what I call living out my dreams.

THE FAITHFULNESS OF JESUS

The Lord Jesus modeled this faithfulness with every step of His life. In the small snapshot of His childhood, we witness a young man with a razor-sharp focus. When His family left Jerusalem, Jesus stayed behind, and they later found Him learning from teachers in the temple. When asked why He stayed behind, the twelve-year-old Savior says, "Did you not know that I must be in my Father's house?" (Luke 2:41–49).

His focus continued. When Satan promised Him authority and glory, Jesus rejected those lies and believed the Word of God. When He began His ministry, He didn't set out to teach the things that would allow Him to rise among the ranks of the religious elite. Instead, He spoke the truth they needed to hear. Jesus was loved by many in His day, but He was hated by many others.

In John 6, after He fed the five thousand, the people tried to force Jesus to be king. They saw His amazing miracles, and they wanted Him to do more. But Jesus saw what they desired, and He withdrew from them. Christ rejected the worldly success they thrust upon Him because He understood that He had a mission. He knew that His kingdom was not of this world. He understood that He had to go to the cross.

At that cross, Jesus died for our glory-seeking and selfish ambition. He died so that we could be saved and realign our goals with His. We must turn away from the lies of the world, and believe the truth of God. The good life is filled with big dreams for the glory of God.

There are brothers and sisters all over the world who will never have the opportunity to be "successful" in the world's eyes. Yet, they're living out their dreams. They were rescued from darkness, and they've been saved in order to proclaim the excellencies of Christ. Their dreams have been informed by His Word, and they just want to be faithful.

So the persecuted pastor in East Asia is living out his dream. He's not rich and his life may end at any moment, but God is using him to build His church. The secretary at the doctor's office is living out her dream. She just wants to do her job well, and love on the people she interacts with every day. I could go on and on. The world wants us to dream small about status and perceived importance. Reject that and dream big.

LYRICS FROM "FANTASY"

You trying to live the dream, ain't you?

The cream, esteem, supreme paper

You thinking it's the place to be, like green acres

Look you live in a dream and I can't even wake you

I know you want that life they all desire

You wanna rise till you can't imagine climbing higher

But that ladder can't stand when it catches fire

And when it stops, you'll be shocked like electric wires

It's cool to like fairy tales

Until you try to live inside of them, that's where we fail

The media pushing death and they do it very well

Man, who woulda thought that obituaries sell?

Look you living in a dream

Open up your eyes, things ain't always what they seem

Reality ain't always what we find upon the screen

They got bait in they hooks and they rhymes full of schemes

It's fantasy

10

GOOD TIMES

RECENTLY I HEARD BAD NEWS about an old friend of mine. He and I were members at the same church, we sang the same songs, and we often read the Word together. Before I knew him, he had been mastered by various types of sexual sin. But he made a commitment to follow Jesus, and he was growing and maturing. The last time we spoke he was still imperfect, but he was fighting to follow Jesus.

But recently I heard he wasn't doing so well. After reaching out to him, I learned that he left the church and reunited with the sinful passions that Jesus died to rid him of. Partying and sex seemed more appealing to him than sweet fellowship with the lover of his soul. Perverted pleasure took the upper hand in his heart, pushing out the longings for pleasures forevermore.

I know that sin's seductive lies tug at my heart every day, and I'm no better than him; but I long to see him fighting his sin and finding his joy in Christ. There's not a single one of us who won't pursue pleasure. The question is: where will we go to find it?

"YOLO"

Lately I've heard a lot of young people use the term "YOLO." It stands for "You only live once." Different people use it at different times, but many seem to use it as a reason to do whatever feels right in the moment. So it may not be the best idea to get drunk tonight, but hey you only live once right? This lie tells us that if it feels right in the moment—it is right.

I don't know if people will still be using that phrase by the time you read this book. But even if people stop saying "YOLO" tomorrow, the faulty worldview will still be there.

Our culture has fed us the lie that feeling good is the highest good. So people are spending their lives in search of a good time, and they'll do whatever it takes to find it. Sleeping around is fine because it feels good. That unhealthy or immoral relationship is fine because, "He makes me happy and that's all that matters." Ignoring your responsibilities is fine because relaxing is more enjoyable.

Our hearts long for something to please us, and our enemy

knows it. You can't even watch TV without being ambushed by pornographic images. Reality TV shows us young people partying and living it up. And if we're honest, sometimes it *does* look like the good life. They're saying loud and clear, "What feels good is good!" In their view, the good life is doing whatever satisfies you in the moment.

This world offers us a lot of opportunities for "pleasure." But if we run after those pleasures above all else, we're aiming too low. The good life is not the life spent pursuing temporal fun, pleasure, and happiness. The good life is a life spent delighting in God and everything He offers us in Christ.

CREATED FOR JOY

Of course I'm not saying that pleasure is wrong. In fact God intended for us to enjoy good things—but on His terms. He created food, and gave us taste buds to enjoy it. He created sex, and means for married couples to be intoxicated with romance.

Adam and Eve experienced perfect pleasure before they disobeyed God. They lived in a world with no sin, no pain, and no corruption. But in Genesis 3, they sinned against God and everything went wrong. After Adam and Eve, all of us are sinners and our defective hearts relate to pleasure in a godless way.

Instead of enjoying God and His creation, we worship pleasure. Instead of looking to God to lead us to pleasure, we turn away from Him to find it on our own terms. This is why pornography has such a strong hold on our generation. Pornography promises the pinnacle of pleasure, and instead it leaves its victims with underwhelming feelings that last for mere minutes.

Instead of believing God and trusting Him to bring us joy, we try building our lives on whatever kind of pleasure we can find down here. But as we trust in Christ and are made more like Him, we can experience pleasure, satisfaction, and joy in the way we were created to.

PSEUDO SATISFACTION

Many of us are still content to spend our lives in pursuit of inferior satisfaction, because we don't know what we're passing up. We know the pleasures we're chasing don't last forever, and we don't really care. But we should.

Imagine waking up one morning with your stomach growling. You're out of food at your house, so you get dressed, rush out the door, and run up the street to get something to quiet your stomach. But instead of going to the grocery store or your favorite restaurant, you go to Foot Locker. You figure, "My stomach is aching . . . so let me grab some new kicks." That sounds ridiculous, right? What on earth would make you think shoes would satisfy your hunger?

This is basically the question God asks in Isaiah 55:2a.

"Why do you spend your money for that which is not bread, and your labor for that which does not satisfy?" God's people were missing the mark. They were passing up God's free offer to quench their hunger and going after costly things that would never truly satisfy them. They were falling in love with idols. An idol is "anything you seek to give you what only God can give."[1] The people in Isaiah were expecting idols to give them satisfaction in a way that only their Creator could. Sadly, all of us have made the same mistake.

We're starving for satisfaction and we're desperately searching for something to quiet our hunger pains. Some of us see the allure of erotic pleasure and we think that's the best there is to offer. We're essentially going to Foot Locker to buy shoes instead of going to Subway for free sandwiches. But shoes can't satisfy our stomach, and sex can't satisfy our souls. We have to start turning away from idols and stop turning down bread.

I'm not only talking about sinful pleasure. We can make the same mistake with good things. For example, marriage is a good, enjoyable gift from God. But if I begin to depend on my wife to satisfy my soul, I'm turning down bread. I'm looking to something for soul satisfaction that was never meant to play that role. Clinging to idols is setting myself up for disappointment and sorrow.

Have you ever seen someone sit down in a chair and break

it? Well the next time that happens, take a break from laughing at them and let it remind you of the truth. Chairs break because they're unable to hold the weight of the person sitting in them. The chair was never meant to hold that much weight. The same could be said of our idols. We look to them to play the role of God, but they were never meant to bear that weight. They will eventually collapse and let us down. Only God can bear the weight of being God.

RICH FOOD

This is why He urges His people in the same verse, Isaiah 55:2b, "Listen diligently to me, and eat what is good, and delight yourselves in rich food." God doesn't want us to go hungry; He wants us to eat the good stuff. Instead of chasing after idols that don't satisfy, God wants us to feast on Him so that our souls would be nourished.

In John 4, Jesus encounters a Samaritan woman getting water from the well. He offers her what He calls living water and tells her why it's superior. "Everyone who drinks of this water will be thirsty again, but whoever drinks of the water that I will give him will never be thirsty again. The water that I will give him will become in him a spring of water welling up to eternal life" (John 4:13–14).

Those who drink from the well of Christ will never thirst again! He can give us the soul satisfaction that we desperately long for. If we receive Christ, we'll be reconnected to the source of all good things. We will be satisfied by Him for an eternity. Often our desire to drink from the wells of this world keeps us from drinking from the wells of Christ. Turn away from those wells and turn to Him.

Only Christ can truly satisfy us because we were made to be satisfied by Him. Cars don't run on water, and human beings aren't truly satisfied by the things of this world. What we need is Christ, and until we drink from Him we won't be truly satisfied.

I know sometimes our pursuits for pleasure aren't the deepest issue. Many of us have been through unbelievable trials and we use futile pleasures as a medicine to cover up pain. All the more reason to run to Jesus! Jesus is a master surgeon of the soul. His all-powerful grace can heal us and give us everlasting joy.

Still there are others of us who run after physical pleasure because we want to be loved. Again, I plead with you to turn to Christ. Momentary pleasure is a lousy substitute for everlasting love. There has never been a love like His and there never will be.

SEEING AND SAVORING

When I read passages like Psalm 63, I'm blown away. In it, David paints a picture of an all-satisfying Lord who is greater than anything we can imagine. No one is begging David to pay attention to God, and no one is dragging him to the sanctuary. Instead, David has this deep-rooted satisfaction in his Creator. He longs for Him, he depends on Him, he thinks about Him as he lies awake at night. He is obsessed with God.

When I was a kid, I used to love watching this Michael Jackson video I had. It had music videos, concert footage, and all kinds of stuff on there. I used to watch that video at least twice a week. I knew all the songs by heart. I'd be in the hallway scuffing up the tile, trying to moonwalk in my dress shoes. When I got home from school, I didn't want to play outside or play board games, I wanted to watch that video. You could say I was obsessed with it. And because I was obsessed with it, I watched it over and over again.

Surely all of us have been obsessed with something in our lifetimes. When we experience something incredible, our hearts latch on. Why did I love that video so much? Because I enjoyed those songs and those videos more than anything else I experienced. They brought me momentary joy.

Well in Psalm 63, David shows us what happens when we taste the goodness of our Creator. He says, "My soul will be satisfied as with fat and rich food" (Psalm 63:5). Compare that with Isaiah 55. When we come to God for satisfaction, there is no disappointment or failure. God is the bread which does satisfy.

In Psalm 63:3 he says, "Because your steadfast love is better than life, my lips will praise you." He considers God's loving-kindness to be better than life itself. That is incredible.

This type of delight in God seems so foreign to us. But this is what happens when we see God for who He is. The clearer we see Him, the more satisfied by Him we are. The more we find our satisfaction in Him, the more we long for more and more.

ENJOYING GOD'S GIFTS

When we experience the pleasures of this world, we will be tempted to latch on to them in an unhealthy way. We'll enjoy them, and our hearts will want to make them ultimate. But we have to fight that urge. When we make those pleasures ultimate, we are believing the lie that God cannot satisfy us as much as they can.

Living by faith in a good God means putting our hearts in check. It means rejecting the idea that worldly pleasure is better than the pleasure God has to offer. It means fighting to believe God's Word over the seductive lies of the Enemy. One of the fruits of the Spirit is self-control. As believers, we are not controlled by our worldly passions. Let our faith in God drive us to self-control.

God has given us many good things to enjoy, but we must enjoy them rightly. God's gifts should lead us to worship

Him. John Piper reminds us that gifts are given to us so that we can use them in a way that shows that gifts are not our treasure, but Christ is. He says, "Seek to make and use money in such a way that Christ looks more important than money."[2] We should enjoy God's gifts but we shouldn't forget the One to whom they're pointing us.

GOOD THINGS FOR BAD PEOPLE

If you're like me, every now and then, the world seems upside down. It seems like those who refuse to submit to God have the best lives. They seem to be having all the fun. It seems like I'm over here denying myself, and they're somewhere popping bottles. In Psalm 73, Asaph lets us into his experience as he feels the exact same way. He vents about the prosperity of the wicked and the trials of the righteous. But eventually He realizes that while the wicked are having a great time now, God's people have something more valuable.

He snaps out of it and says these beautiful words, "Whom have I in heaven but you? And there is nothing on earth that I desire besides you. My flesh and my heart may fail, but God is the strength of my heart and my portion forever" (Psalm 73:25–26). Once we see God for who He is, the spoils of this world will seem worthless. All of our other loves will fall into their proper place as we bow before the all-satisfying God of glory.

THE JOY OF JESUS

If ever there was a man who wasn't driven by worldly pleasure, it was Jesus. He wasn't an ascetic who denied Himself any enjoyment, but He enjoyed God's good gifts in the right way. He didn't worship them above God; He used them to glorify God. This is most clearly evident when He is tempted by Satan to break His fast. Instead, He calls on God's Word and rejects Satan's offer (Luke 4:1–12). Of course bread isn't wrong, but Christ chose the will of the Father over satisfying His stomach.

At the end of His life, Jesus denied Himself momentary joy for eternal joy. Hebrews 12:2 says He endured the cross "for the joy that was set before him." Christ knew the eternal joy He would experience in glory, in fellowship with the Father and the Spirit. He knew the joy that would come from restoring sinners to God. And His focus on that joy led Him to endure the pain that came with His death on the cross. Let us follow in His example.

As believers, we may have to deny ourselves temporary joys for a season. But ultimately, we are never trading in joy for sorrow. Rather, we're trading the pleasure we have now that's fleeting, for an eternal joy that will last forever. At times, the good life means turning down minutes or months of pleasure. But the good news is we trade it in for "pleasures forevermore" (Psalm 16:11).

LYRICS FROM "FANTASY"

Welcome to the real world

Where there's real treasure, real pearls

Those who try to gain the world only lose souls

And chasing fools goals only gets you fools gold

Welcome to the good life, where there's real joy

Now that old life seems like a killjoy

It's ironic that the life giver was killed boy

He rose and He chose me, you know He fills a real void

We were made to be connected to the life giver

To build our life around Him, with His life in us

But our pride likes to rise, them lies get us

They separate us from the good, we despise Scripture

But we can turn back, to the forever source

The one who can't be described by my metaphors

Even if I'm poor, I'm rich if I let Him set the course

At his right hand are pleasures forevermore[3]

SECTION IV:

WHAT KIND OF GOOD
WILL GOD GIVE ME?

11

GOOD EXPECTATIONS

I'VE HEARD IT SAID THAT ALL frustration comes from unmet expectation. We expect things to go one way but they end up another way, therefore we end up frustrated. Here's an example:

In 2010 NBA star, LeBron James, left the Cleveland Cavaliers and took his talents to South Beach. After saying farewell to his former team in an overhyped ESPN special, the Miami Heat's new "big three" threw a televised celebration to make sure everybody knew they were God's gift to basketball. During this TV special LeBron infamously set the bar pretty high, promising a championship or two . . . or eight. The team accomplished quite a bit their first season, but fell short of a championship.

Despite the fact that this brand-new, cut and pasted Miami squad made it all the way to the finals, they were still looked at as failures until they finally got that ring. Why? Because the expectations were so high. The high level of talent, plus the big promises led fans to be dissatisfied with a measly Eastern Conference championship. They expected the team to win it all, and they would accept no less. On the other hand, if one of the worst teams in the league would have simply made it to the first round of the playoffs, their fans would have been ecstatic.

Expectations influence our responses pretty dramatically. Forget about NBA championships though. What about our expectations from God? Our response to what He does in our lives will depend on what we expect from Him. The good life is lived in eager expectation of the good things God has promised His people.

TRUE FAITH

There are few things that infuriate me more than preachers lying about God. Preachers are supposed to speak on behalf of God, but many of them hold out promises to their people that God never made. So when churchgoers don't receive all the blessings that their pastors promised them, their faith is damaged. They're convinced that God went back on His Word. But the Lord is faithful, and never breaks a promise. He is worthy of every ounce of our faith.

Faith is often misunderstood. Many people think faith means believing God will give us whatever we need or desire. So if we think we really need to get a new job, faith is believing that God will make that happen for us. If we really want a spouse, faith is believing that God will bring us one. But unless God has promised something to us, we can't lay claim to it or be mad at God when He doesn't deliver. Faith isn't believing God will give you everything you want. <u>Faith is believing that God will do as He promised</u>.

If you look at Hebrews 11:1 it says, "faith is the assurance of things hoped for . . ." But this doesn't mean the assurance of any random thing we want and hope for. If you look through the examples of faith in Hebrews 11, those saints hoped for things God had promised them. Even though they couldn't see them yet, they believed and obeyed God. They knew their faithful God would keep His promises.

So what are the promises that we can lay claim to? First we should establish who God has made promises to. God has not promised to prosper, watch over, or bless those who rebel against Him. Not everyone is a child of God, and therefore not everyone can lay claim to the promises of the Father. Every good thing you have is from God (James 1:17), but God doesn't promise to give good things to all of us.

If you haven't repented of your sin, the only thing you've

been promised is judgment. But those who receive Christ by faith become the children of God (John 1:12). And God has made many great promises to His children.

NOT GUILTY

Romans 8 is one of the sweetest chapters in all of Scripture. In it we find the most precious promises God has given to His people. It begins with one of the hardest to believe. "There is therefore now no condemnation for those who are in Christ Jesus" (Romans 8:1). Because Christ was condemned for us, we can never be condemned.

Later in the passage, Paul asks the question, "Who shall bring any charge against God's elect? It is God who justifies. Who is to condemn? Christ Jesus is the one who died—more than that, who was raised—who is at the right hand of God, who indeed is interceding for us" (Romans 8:33–34).

We've all committed crimes against our Creator. There are witnesses, there's video surveillance footage, and we left fingerprints at the scene. It's abundantly clear that we're guilty. Yet no one can bring a single charge against us. Why? Because the Judge has declared us, in Christ, as "not guilty." We're seen as righteous before God.

The only final judgment that matters is God's and He's declared us "not guilty." This isn't to say that we no longer sin, but He's promised that when we stand before Him, we'll be acquitted of our crimes. Christ is the sacrifice who took the punishment for our sins, and now He's the attorney who intercedes for us.

Don't ever let anyone hold your sins against you. Satan can't declare you guilty, though he would love to. We must ignore him when he says that God could never forgive sinners like you and me. The bitter people in your life can't declare you guilty because you've been forgiven. <u>Repent of the ways you've sinned against them and give it over to God</u>. Even *you* can't declare you guilty. Our sin often weighs us down, but we must remember that those sins have been paid for. We've been given an eternal "not guilty" verdict and it can't be overturned. There are no appeals.

COHEIRS

There are some celebrities who are loved and others who are hated. Some of the most commonly hated celebrities are those who are rich and famous for no reason. America always loves a good rags-to-riches story about hard work and its rewards. But that's not these rich people. These rich people were born into wealthy and famous families, and all they do is reap the benefits. People look down on them because the rest of us have to work hard for every cent, while they enjoy the luxuries of someone else's hard work.

The believer actually has something in common with

these folks. Not financially, but spiritually. We are spiritually spoiled. We've been given "every spiritual blessing" and not an ounce of it is due to our work. We'll spend an eternity riding on the coattails of Christ and benefitting from His work on the cross. Of course His work moves us to change our lifestyle, but we've earned nothing from God. Everything we have is from grace.

We receive everything that Jesus earned. We are coheirs with Him. Though we behaved like rebels, God has promised us the inheritance that Jesus deserves. Though we deserve to be judged, we will reign with Christ. We will inherit eternal life.

God has also promised us His Spirit. The same Spirit that raised Jesus from the dead dwells inside our feeble frames. Without the Spirit of God, none of us would be able to come to Christ, understand the Word, or obey a single command. We would have no spiritual gifts, our evangelism would be powerless, and our prayers would be pointless. The Spirit of God gives us every ounce of spiritual vitality that we have. We do not get to walk with Jesus in the same way the disciples did, but we've been given something just as amazing.

GOD IS FOR US

My dad used to tell me stories about his upbringing all the time. By his account, he was always liked by everybody. Even though he wasn't a tough guy, nobody could mess with him because he was cool with the tough guys. One of his friends was a big, swole, Deebo-like dude. So whenever anybody had problems with my dad, this mammoth young man had my dad's back. Because the big dude was on his side, my dad had no worries.

God has promised His people that He is for them, and when God is for you, nobody can realistically be against you. Nobody and nothing can even come in your vicinity without permission from the sovereign God of the universe. It's kind of like showing up to every pickup game with Michael Jordan. Who could ever beat you? Well as a Christian you show up to every situation with the God of the Universe as your Father. He is for us and we are on His side.

ALL GOOD THINGS

If someone said they would give you everything they have access to, what would you say? If they said they'd give you their money, their home, their car, their job, etc. You would say, "Yeah, right. Prove it." Well God has promised in <u>Romans 8:32 that He will give His people all things</u>. But we can't say, "Yeah, right. Prove it," because He already has.

He's already given His Son, that which is most valuable to Him. So questioning Him is silly. He's proven His willingness to give freely to those whom He loves. We should never assume that God is unwilling to give us anything good. It's almost like He's already given us a million dollars, and we question whether or not He'll give us fifty cents.

Though sometimes, we twist biblical promises like this into "God will give me all things that I want." That's not what the text is saying. The Bible is clear that God will only give His children good things. So God will give us absolutely anything—unless it's not what's best for us.

SUFFERING IN THE GOOD LIFE

We should also not mistake "give us all good things" for "not allow us to suffer." God does not promise us that this life will be free from suffering. Don't believe those preachers who say the Christian life is a life free from any pain or worry. Christ did purchase a pain-free life for us, but we won't experience that until the next life. We don't experience every blessing of the cross on this side of heaven.

In fact, God promised that we will suffer as Christians. Suffering is part of our calling. Suffering is part of the good life. "For to this you have been called, because Christ also suffered for you, leaving you an example, so that you might follow in his steps" (1 Peter 2:21). "We are . . . fellow heirs with Christ, provided we suffer with him in order that we may also be glorified with him" (Romans 8:16–17). "Share in suffering as a good soldier of Christ Jesus" (2 Timothy 2:3). "For it has been granted to you that for the sake of Christ you should not only believe in him but also suffer for his sake" (Philippians 1:29). The New Testament is filled with verses like these.

Some of us may suffer from disease or injury. Others of us may lose our jobs and suffer poverty. Others of us will suffer from broken families and relationships. All of us will, in some way, be persecuted for our faith in Christ. The good life isn't easy, but it's worth it. God uses that suffering for our good and His glory.

Once again, we have to define "good" the way God does. God can take the most unlikely things and use them for good in our lives. While our main goal is often comfort, God has other goals in mind. His primary goal is His own glory. But God also uses our suffering to make us more like Christ. Hebrews 12:11 says, "For the moment all discipline seems painful rather than pleasant, but later it yields the peaceful fruit of righteousness to those who have been trained by it." Complaining to God about our suffering is like complaining to our trainers about our workouts. Yes it hurts, but He's doing it to make us stronger.

Even our greatest enemy, death, can be turned for our good. Death was once a frightening enemy. But Christ has turned it into a friend. Death is now a doorway to take us to our faithful lover, Christ. Nothing can hurt us.

The difference between a Christian and a non-Christian is not that one suffers and the other doesn't. The difference is a Christian always wins. The Christian can never lose. Whatever comes our way, we still win! Paul calls us more than conquerors (Romans 8:37).

I remember playing Super Mario Brothers and loving it when I got the blinking star. When Mario got that star and started blinking, he was invincible! His enemies could touch him but they couldn't kill him. In a similar fashion, our enemies can touch us and they can even hurt us. But they can't defeat us.

This changes the way we live our lives. We play the game differently when we know the outcome in advance. It allows us to be fearless. We don't fear those who can kill the body because they can't kill the soul. We fear God alone.

OMNIPOTENT LOVE

The promise in Romans 8 that I cling to most is the promise that nothing can separate us from the love of God in Christ. Our Creator loves His people with a sovereign, omnipotent, unstoppable love. Look what Paul does: he goes through a list of the most terrible things we can possibly imagine, and says even those can't separate us from the love of God in Christ. "Who shall separate us from the love of Christ? Shall tribulation, or distress, or persecution, or famine, or nakedness, or danger, or sword?" (Romans 8:35).

A few verses later he says, "For I am sure that neither death nor life, nor angels nor rulers, nor things present nor things to come, nor powers, nor height nor depth, nor anything else in all creation, will be able to separate us from the love of God in Christ Jesus our Lord" (Romans 8:38–39).

That is incredible. Even marriage vows say, "Till death do us part." But not even death can separate us from the love of God in Christ Jesus. Divorce, persecution, rape, death—all of them are powerless to separate you from the love of God. The most important thing about believers is that we are in Christ. And absolutely nothing can change that.

HALL OF FAITH

The writer of Hebrews gives us portraits of some of the greatest among God's people throughout history. This list includes Moses, Abraham, Sarah, and many more. What each of these saints has in common is an imperfect, yet abiding faith in the God of their salvation.

God made promises to them, and they believed those promises. Their faith in His promises changed the way they lived their lives. Abraham left his home for a land he'd never seen. Noah built an ark though he saw no evidence of this great storm. God's people walked through the dry ground as the Red Sea was split. The list could go on and on. Most of these people died without seeing all of God's promises come to pass. Yet, as the text says, they were awaiting a better city that God had promised. Their lives were full of victories and losses. But losses in this life are really just delayed victories, because we win in the end.

Their faith in the promises of God allowed them to live fearless lives of faith. They were able to throw caution to the wind and run after their God. If you want another example of what the good life looks like, look at these people. They lived by faith in a good God.

This is what I want for you, family. I want you to be able to ignore lies and live in light of the promises of God. When it looks like all is lost, I want you to trust in God's promises. When life hurts, I want you to cling to the truth that suffering can't separate you from the love of God. When family, or even your own reason, tells you that God is lying, I want you to trust God. He will definitely keep His promises.

And as for the life free from any suffering, pain, or hardship God has promised us? That will come later. I assure you, there will be no disappointment when we receive from God what He has promised us.

LYRICS FROM "FOR MY GOOD"

He ain't gon' give me nothing
If it ain't good for me
Sometimes I ask for something
That's seeming good to me
But my God is wiser
It's clear He really loves me
Sometimes He tells me no
If not it would be ugly
How I'm gon' question Him?
Deny my rest in Him?
He'll give us all things
He gave His Son who bled for sin
My Lord is more than good, it's clear that He delights to give
Good gifts to His sons and daughters, all those who in
Christ are His

For my good
You did it all for my good
You never put so much on me that I couldn't take it
I know I can make it
Cause everything's gon' be ok
It's all good.[1]

12

THE FOREVER GOOD LIFE

"IMAGINE THERE'S NO HEAVEN, it's easy if you try. No hell below us, above us only sky. Imagine all the people living for today."[1]

Those lyrics are from a John Lennon song called "Imagine." He paints a picture of a world where there is no heaven or hell, and everybody is living for today. I assume he wanted us to imagine a beautiful world where everyone lives in perfect harmony. But instead, the picture he paints is a frightening one. If today is all we have to live for, that is a frightening existence.

Now I want you to read another quote. There's another John, the apostle, who wants us to imagine a different type of world, a future world he saw in a vision.

Then I saw a new heaven and a new earth, for the first heaven and the first earth had passed away, and the sea was no more. And I saw the holy city, new Jerusalem, coming down out of heaven from God, prepared as a bride adorned for her husband. And I heard a loud voice from the throne saying, "Behold, the dwelling place of God is with man. He will dwell with them, and they will be his people, and God himself will be with them as their God. He will wipe away every tear from their eyes, and death shall be no more, neither shall there be mourning, nor crying, nor pain anymore, for the former things have passed away." And he who was seated on the throne said, "Behold, I am making all things new" (Revelation 21:1–5).

HEAVEN

Heaven is a popular idea in our culture. People talk about heaven as a place where we will all go when we die. It's a dreamy destination where we strap on angel wings, reunite with our families, and hang out forever. The hip-hop legend Tupac famously wondered if there was a heaven for a gangster. He even described his picture of heaven in a song called "Thugz Mansion."

I think the reason our culture longs for heaven is because we all know this world is messed up. There's something inside of us that recognizes this isn't how it's supposed to be.

All of us wish we could go to a place where everything is right.

Well the culture is not all wrong about heaven. This life is not the end for us. There's not a single human being that stops existing when their life on earth stops. The culture is also right in believing that heaven exists and it's a glorious place. But heaven is not like a country club where everybody eventually gets a membership. Heaven is the eternal resting place for those who have lived their lives by faith in a good God, in Jesus. The good life is fully realized when God's people are raised to spend eternal life with our Savior.

When sin entered into the world everything changed. Death came into the picture. All of creation came under bondage. The result is sinful man, disease, natural disasters, and a whole host of other evils. It's hard to imagine a life free from these things because it's all we've ever known. All of it came into our world because of sin, but there's good news. The Bible teaches that one day God will make all things new. This is the vision John saw in Revelation 21. It's like God let John turn to the final pages and see the conclusion of the story.

WHAT WILL IT BE LIKE?

As John describes, heaven will come down to Earth and God will dwell with His people. God will restore His reign in all of creation. He will do away with all evil and His people will live in absolute paradise. There will be no more sin. There will be no more death. There will be no more sickness. There will be no more pain or suffering. Everything that Jesus purchased for us on the cross will be there for us. God will not hold back any good things from His people.

Some of us suffer from physical ailments. Those ailments will be a thing of the past. We'll be given new, perfect bodies. Others of us walk around with the pain of past abuse. All the sorrow from past experience will be erased. Others of us have been plagued by mental weakness. That too will be erased and our minds will be sharper than ever. We will no longer struggle with sin. We will perfectly glorify our Savior forever. We will be like Him (1 John 3:2).

There are many good things we've enjoyed on this Earth, but they are just the beginning. The joys we experience in this life are just mere shadows, pointing to a glorious reality. The pleasures in heaven will far surpass anything we enjoyed on this Earth. It is truly impossible to exaggerate the glories we will experience for an eternity.

WITH GOD

The most amazing part of John's vision is that God dwells with His people. The most devastating effect of our sin is that it separates us from God. We've been reconciled to Him and we'll get to spend eternity with Him! God's people will no longer live by faith. We will live by sight! "For now we see in a mirror dimly, but then face to face. Now I know in part; then I shall know fully, even as I have been fully known" (1 Corinthians 13:12).

We will no longer have to settle for what we've heard about Christ. We will see Him with our very own eyes. And we will worship Him forever. We won't fight for our own glory anymore, because it will be abundantly clear that the glory belongs to Him. We will sing along with the angels, "Holy, holy, holy is the Lord!" And we will magnify His glory in all that we do.

THE BEST LIFE

I remember being a kid and thinking, "I'd love to go to heaven, but I hope I don't die before I get rich and get married." Silly thoughts like that make it pretty clear that I had no idea what heaven is like. My childish perspective was the opposite of Paul's perspective. He says, "My desire is to depart and be with Christ, for that is far better" (Philippians 1:23). Paul understood that it is far better to be with Jesus than to be here on this Earth.

We too should long to be home to be with our Lord. There should be nothing more attractive to us than being with Christ. For believers, heaven is our true home. Those who are living by faith in a good God understand that this life isn't the main event. The life we live now is merely a preview of the one to come. One day we will be with Christ in paradise. And it lasts forever.

HOW DO WE GET THERE?

Contrary to much of what our culture says, heaven is not the place everybody goes to when they die. Jesus says in the gospel of John that all of us will be raised, "those who have done good to the resurrection of life, and those who have done evil to the resurrection of judgment" (John 5:29). Those who lived by faith in Christ will be raised to eternal life in heaven with Him. But those who lived a life of rebellion against God will be judged. They will spend eternity in hell. Only those who loved Christ in this life will experience His love for all of eternity. If you haven't been reunited to God, I plead with you to put your faith in Jesus. Only He can save us and give us eternal life.

HEAVENLY MINDED

I've heard many people say that we should not be "so heavenly minded that we're of no earthly good." What they mean is, don't be so focused on heaven that you don't care about this life. I can understand that. But a proper focus on heaven makes us more fruitful in this life, not the other way around.

When we understand that this life is not all there is, we can give of ourselves freely. We can grind now because we get to rest later. We can give our money away, knowing that we're storing up treasures in heaven. We endure suffering because we know it's just "light momentary affliction" (2 Corinthians

4:17). We can follow God, even to the grave, knowing that we will be raised to eternal life. That's what I call the good life.

LYRICS FROM "TAKE ME THERE"

Hey I don't know about you but I can't wait till the day
When I'll be with my Lord and everything is ok
And I'll be just like Him so my sin ain't in the way
Basking in His glory, that's where I'll wanna stay
A place where shadows give way to the real
And circumstances can't change the way that I feel
Joy in my Savior that Satan can't steal
Because he's been defeated, yeah you know the deal
The real good life, I can't wait please take me soon
Until then I'll be praising in the waiting room
Fighting by His grace
Can't wait to embrace the Groom, until then I'm like . . .

I just wanna go where
I'm only breathing your air
Father hear my prayer
Take me there, take me there
I just wanna see you
Brighter than I'm used to
Finally seeing clear
Take me there, take me there, take me there[2]

SHARING THE GOOD LIFE **WITH OTHERS**

THERE ARE SOME PEOPLE who grow up in rough neighborhoods with nothing to their names. But then they find some way to make a ton of money. So they move out, and never think about their neighborhoods again. All they care about is taking care of themselves. They never give back to the community, and they never think about the kids growing up like they did. They are criticized as self-centered snobs who forgot where they came from.

Well I'm afraid that many believers have become spiritual self-centered snobs. Many of us have forgotten where we came from. As Ephesians 2:1–2 reminds us, "You were dead in your trespasses and sins in which you once walked . . . " There was a time when all of us were hopelessly lost in our

sins and far from God. The only reason any of us are reconnected to God is the grace of God.

If you are a Christian today, it's not because you've met
some list of requirements, and therefore have found a way to
restore yourself to God. That's the beautiful thing about the
Christian gospel. It tells us that God loves us, pursues us, and
woos us back to Himself. He sees our need. He sees our weakness. He sees our sin; and He does the reconciling. Jesus had
compassion on us, literally came to get us, picked us up, and
carried us to God. Our legs were lame and our hearts were
hard, but Jesus brought us to the Father. But you never would
have known about this Jesus if nobody told you about Him.

There are other people who are back where you used to be.
They're dead in their trespasses and sins. They're not living
the good life, in fact, they're rebelling against it. They need
to be saved, to turn from their sin and believe the good news
about Jesus.

GOD'S PLAN

Look at what Paul says in 2 Corinthians 5:19, "in Christ
God was reconciling the world to himself, not counting their
trespasses against them, and entrusting to us the message of
reconciliation."

God has a plan to reconcile sinners from all over the world
to Himself. Not just you and me, but many others—others on

our campuses, others in our families, people on other con-tinents. God has decreed that He will do this through Christ. And He's done this at great cost to Himself. He gave His Son to do it.

So when you see people on the street, people on your campus, what do you think of them? Do you see them as an annoyance? Do you ignore them? Or do you enjoy them, but ignore the fact that they have eternal souls?

You should think of them as men and women made in the image of God. They are people who God loves, but who need to be reconciled to Him and raised to life. Anyone can be rec-onciled. Some people think only old white dudes in suits and black grandmothers with church hats can be saved. Nope! "Everyone who calls on the name of the Lord will be saved" (Romans 10:13). We should never look at a person and assume God can't save them. He can. There is no obstacle that can stand in His way, and there is no enemy that can stop Him.

God has a plan to save sinners and He will carry it out. The question is: how?

GOD'S GIFT

Well let's look at those verses again. In 2 Corinthians 5:18 he says, "[God], through Christ reconciled us to himself and gave us the ministry of reconciliation . . ." Paul says that God has not only reconciled him, but that He's given him the message of reconciliation. And this is true, not only of Paul and Timothy, and not only of the Corinthian church, but of everyone who God has reconciled to Himself. If you've been reconciled to God, you have now been made a minister of reconciliation—a servant of reconciliation.

And it should shock us that God would do such a thing, especially if we think about Paul. He was not always a nice guy. When we first meet Paul in the book of Acts, he isn't a Christian. He's a persecutor of Christians. He was an enemy of the gospel, yet God saved him and made him part of the team. He took one of the foremost opponents of the gospel, stopped him in his tracks, saved him, and used him to spread the gospel.

This would almost be like President Obama finding Osama Bin Laden, but deciding not to treat him like an enemy and to instead make him a member of his presidential cabinet. It would be absurd and unexpected if the very one who's done our country so much harm was used to help carry out our plans. Well Jesus took Paul, who was an enemy of the gospel and persecutor of Christians, and turned him into a servant of the gospel. And God has taken sinners like you and me, who spurned the gospel, and has made us ministers of the gospel as well. That is a testimony to God's one-of-a- kind, unique grace and transforming power.

God doesn't need us, yet He has allowed us to participate in His sovereign plan to reconcile sinners to Himself. We get to be a part of His grand plan of redemption, and that is a privilege. Not because we deserve to, but because He is gracious.

This is one of the major ways all believers have been called to serve. We are to be ministers of the gospel. You may or may not be an evangelist. But whether or not you actually are passionate about seeing other sinners reconciled—that ministry has been given to you. So what should that ministry look like for us?

Well look down at 2 Corinthians 5:19. It says, "that is, in Christ God was reconciling the world to himself, not counting their trespasses against them, and entrusting to us the message of reconciliation." We see from this verse that giving us the ministry is synonymous with entrusting us with the message. Sharing the message you have been entrusted with is at the heart of what it means to be a minister.

It becomes even clearer in verse 20. "Therefore, we are ambassadors for Christ, God making his appeal through us. We implore you on behalf of Christ, be reconciled to God" (2 Corinthians 5:20).

Paul says that we are ambassadors for Christ. An ambassador is "an authorized representative or messenger."[1] So we are God's representatives, sent by Him, to interact with others on His behalf. So we are God's representatives, sent by Him to interact with others on His behalf.

Christian, you are no longer a regular guy or girl. Your

identity has been changed. You are not a civilian anymore. You're an ambassador and you've been given a mission. God is at work in the world and He's called you to join Him.

GOD'S MESSENGERS

As messengers sent by God, our role is simple. It's not to make people think we're cool; we can be tempted to do this at times. But you don't have to convince people you're like them before you can call them to be transformed by Jesus. That's not our role and that's not where our power comes from. Our goal is to plead with others on God's behalf. God makes appeals to sinners, and He does it through sinners He's already saved. He appeals through us. We're like mailmen delivering important letters. We're like carrier pigeons with a precious message attached. We're witnesses testifying about what we've seen.

We're like language translators. The translator's value is in listening, and then relaying what they've heard. It's not about what they can add; it's about accurately relaying the message. The same goes for the evangelist. Our task is to share what we've heard.

UNIVERSAL CALLING

The truth is that none of us evangelize near as much as we should. It's because we are apathetic, or ashamed, or self-conscious. We need to confess that sin, ask for forgiveness, turn from that sin, and obey God in this area. Don't beat yourself up, just repent and ask God for grace to do better.

Somebody might say, "But that's not my gifting. I'm better at serving behind the scenes. I have the gifts of service and hospitality." Well to you I'd say you're called to do both. One of the ways you've been called to serve is by sharing Christ with others.

Or you might say, "But I'm not that eloquent." Well eloquence is not the power of God for salvation. The gospel is. So you don't have to be Billy Graham, you just need to tell people what the good news is. The same good news we talked about in chapter four is the very message God uses to save. All you need to do is proclaim that message.

Or someone might be thinking, "I'm not ready yet." Maybe you're a new Christian and you feel like you don't have all the answers. Well you don't have to have all the answers. Talk with other believers who can help you understand the gospel better, and can help you find simple ways to share it with others.

One time I was doing a concert and sharing the gospel at a prison. After I shared the gospel, I told the prisoners they could talk to me afterwards if they wanted to know more about Christ. After it was all over, one of the chaplains came up to me and rebuked me. He said, "Don't you ever share the gospel without giving people a chance to respond! You didn't give an invitation, man!"

I thought for a minute. After a while I was reminded of Acts 10:44. It says, "While Peter was still saying these things, the Holy Spirit fell on all who heard the word." God didn't need an altar call to save anyone. The gospel itself is the invitation. The gospel calls us to turn and believe. God's Spirit works when the good news is preached.

We rob God of glory when we put too much stock in our evangelistic methods. We do the same when we assume we aren't eloquent enough to evangelize. Don't put all the responsibility on yourself. God reconciles, we implore. God saves, we plead. God redeems, we proclaim. We call folks to repent and believe, and God works it in hearts. We've just got to be faithful to what God has called us to do.

The message that you have to share with others is mind blowing. You are a messenger with good news! Let's act like it. Let's look for opportunities to share. We should be strategically finding ways to share Christ with others—when you are home for Christmas, when you pass by homeless folks, when you hang with friends in school. Be gracious and loving, but be bold.

I can think of many times I've shared the gospel in a very similar way with different people. Sometimes they receive it and sometimes they reject it. This could lead to deep discouragement, but I know God hasn't called me to produce responses. He hasn't called me to save anybody. He's called me to tell them about the Savior who can.

DON'T KEEP IT TO YOURSELF

In Texas we celebrate "Juneteenth." On January 1, 1863, Abraham Lincoln's emancipation proclamation became effective. But it had almost no effect in the southern states, at least not right away. Most of the slaves were still slaves. They had no idea that they had been free for over two years. But on June 19, 1865, General Gordon Granger arrived in Galveston, Texas, with good news. He said, "The people of Texas are informed that, in accordance with a proclamation from the Executive of the United States, all slaves are free."[2]

Now could you imagine General Granger keeping that news to himself? Of course not. You and I know many people in bondage. We have the good news that can set them free.

Let's not keep it from them.

SPECIAL THANKS

I'M GRATEFUL TO GOD for this opportunity to point others to His truth. And I'm thankful to God for all the people He's put in my life to help me through the process.

Thank you to my wife, Jessica, for once again allowing me to devote so much time to a project. Thank you to everyone who encouraged me to write. I wouldn't have attempted this if God hadn't put you in my life. Thank you to everyone who read over the book and gave input. You helped make it so much better.

Thank you to all the men who've poured into me over the years. You've deeply influenced the way I think about God, His Word, and His world.

Thank you to Moody for helping make this happen. Thank

you to Reach for helping to build the platform. Thank you to everyone who's supported me over the years. And thank You, Lord, for whatever fruit will come from this feeble attempt. Glory to God alone.

NOTES

Chapter 1: Don't Eat the Fruit
1. "Money Ain't a Thing," © 1998 by Jermaine Dupri, Shawn Carter, Steve Arrington, Charles Carter, Buddy Hank, Roger Parker (Atlanta: Crosswire Studios).

2. "Robot," © 2012 by Trip Lee (Atlanta: Reach Records).

Chapter 2: The Good Teacher
1. "Robot," © 2012 by Trip Lee (Atlanta: Reach Records).

Chapter 3: A New Definition
1. "Good Life," © 2007 by Kanye West, Faheem Najm, James Ingram, Quincy Jones, Adrian Davis (New York: Def Jam Recordings, Roc-A-Fella Records).

2. "New Dreams," © 2012 by Trip Lee (Atlanta: Reach Records).

Chapter 4: The Good News
1. James I. Packer, *God's Plans for You* (Wheaton: Crossway Books, 2001), 44.

2. "Jesus Is Alive," © 2008 by Shai Linne (Philadelphia: Lamp Mode Recordings).

3. "Love on Display," © 2012 by Trip Lee (Atlanta: Reach Records).

Chapter 5: The Good Book
1. "Know Me," © 2012 by Trip Lee (Atlanta: Reach Records).

Chapter 6: Good People
1. Mark Dever, *The Church: The Gospel Made Visible* (Nashville: B&H Academic, 2012), 3.

2. "Go to Church," © 2006 by Snoop Dogg, Lil Jon, Ice Cube, C. Love, J. Phillips, (Encino, CA: Da Lench Mob).

3. "Good People," © 2012 by Trip Lee. (Atlanta: Reach Records).

Chapter 7: Good Works
1. "Robot," © 2012 by Trip Lee (Atlanta: Reach Records).

Chapter 8: Good Stuff
1. "Heart Problem," © 2012 by Trip Lee (Atlanta: Reach Records).

Chapter 9: Good Dreams
1. "Fantasy," © 2012 by Trip Lee (Atlanta: Reach Records).

Chapter 10: Good Times
1. Timothy Keller, *Counterfeit Gods: The Empty Promises of Money, Sex, and Power* (New York: Dutton Books, 2009), 7.

2. John Piper, September 4, 2010, "How Can I Glorify God on the Job?," *Desiring God Blog*, www.desiringgod.org/blog/posts/how-can-i-glorify-god-on-the-job.

3. "Fantasy," © 2012 by Trip Lee (Atlanta: Reach Records).

Chapter 11: Good Expectations
1. "For My Good," © 2012 by Trip Lee (Atlanta: Reach Records).

Chapter 12: The Forever Good Life
1. "Imagine," © 1971 by John Lennon (London: Apple).

2. "Take Me There," © 2012 by Trip Lee (Atlanta: Reach Records).

Appendix: Sharing the Good Life with Others

1. Merriam Webster Dictionary, www.merriam-webster.com/dictionary/ambassador.

2. "The History of Juneteenth," JUNETEENTH.com, last revised May 31, 2012, http://www.juneteenth.com/history.htm.

EXCLUSIVE OFFER
AT THEGOODLIFETHEBOOK.COM

Stories are best told by those who have been impacted by truth. In *The Good Life* audio book, narrated by Trip Lee, he unveils the truth about the *The Good Life*. It's within our reach, and yet beyond anything this world has to offer. Find out how you can **receive your copy of the audio book & NEW MUSIC by Trip Lee** (5 songs with all new exclusive content) at www.TheGoodLifeTheBook.com!

Get your audio book and music today!

Also available as an eBook

MOODY
PUBLISHERS

www.MoodyPublishers.com

STANDARD DATA RATES MAY APPLY

THE GOOD LIFE CD

Get it at **reachrecords.com**

Other Trip Lee Music